MRS
KEPPEL

MRS
KEPPEL

—Mistress to the King—

Tom Quinn

Biteback Publishing

First published in Great Britain in 2016 by
Biteback Publishing Ltd
Westminster Tower
3 Albert Embankment
London SE1 7SP
Copyright © Tom Quinn 2016

ISBN 978-1-78590-048-8

10 9 8 7 6 5 4 3 2 1

A CIP catalogue record for this book is available from the British Library.

Set in Adobe Caslon Pro by Adrian McLaughlin

Printed and bound in Great Britain by
CPI Group (UK) Ltd, Croydon CR0 4YY

'More knowledge may be gained of a man's real character by a short conversation with one of his servants than from a formal and studied narrative begun with his pedigree and ended with his funeral.'
—SAMUEL JOHNSON, *THE RAMBLER*

'Alice Keppel had the sexual morals of an alley cat.'
—VICTORIA GLENDINNING

'She [Alice Keppel] has had her fists in the money-bags these fifty years…'
—VIRGINIA WOOLF'S DIARY

Contents

Prelude:
Then and Now

*A*BOVE ALL THINGS Alice Keppel loved money and position, and it was these loves that motivated her to climb the social ladder into the highly lucrative position of the King's favourite mistress. Three generations later, Alice's great-granddaughter, Camilla Parker Bowles, followed in her footsteps when she became the lover of Charles, Prince of Wales, at catastrophic cost to Charles's marriage to Lady Diana Spencer.

Camilla Shand, as she then was, grew up in an atmosphere in which affairs were treated much as her great-grandmother Alice Keppel's circle treated them: they were private matters with no moral aspect at all. And thus when Camilla said to Charles in 1970, 'My great-grandmother was the mistress of your great-great-grandfather, so how about it?' she no doubt simply thought this was carrying on an exciting upper-class tradition; a tradition that says morality, like taxes, is for little people.

Camilla's affair with Charles continued before, during and after his marriage to Diana Spencer, and Camilla even helped Charles buy Highgrove House, still his home today, because it was close to the house she shared with her husband. It was a shrewd move of which Camilla's great-grandmother would have approved.

Knowing that as a divorced woman she would not be allowed to marry Charles, Camilla advised him to marry Lady Diana Spencer. The perception was that Diana was timid, easily led and therefore unlikely to make a fuss when she discovered that Charles had no intention of giving up his mistress.

Diana was to become Charles's 'brood mare', just as Queen Alexandra had been his great-great-grandfather's brood mare. Camilla played the role of her own great-grandmother Alice Keppel, who was described at the time as a key figure in Edward VII's 'loose box'.

Camilla's affair with Charles was aided and abetted by an upper-class set that, in its attitudes and morals, is largely unchanged since Edwardian times. It's a world closed to outsiders with its own rules and its own fierce desire to protect those on the inside. It relies heavily on the deference paid to it by politicians and the governing classes. It is the set centred on a few dozen large country estates still privately owned by ancient families. Social mobility via great wealth allows no admittance to this world even today – foreigners are still seen as outsiders just as the Cassels and Rothschilds were seen as outsiders in the late nineteenth and early twentieth centuries.

It was this group of aristocrats, a group that overlaps with those who helped Lord Lucan on the night he killed the family nanny, that enabled Charles and Camilla to pursue their affair by meeting each other at the country houses of their friends; friends who would never dream of letting anyone outside their circle know what was going on. They would have known, too, about the plan to find Charles a complacent wife. Then and now they live as their ancestors lived a century ago. The only difference is that the broughams and phaetons have become Range Rovers and Bentleys.

These are families who find it absurd that there are still people in the world who live on less than half a million a year; they laugh at the idea that there are people who have to buy their own furniture (rather than inheriting it) or cook their own food. They still defer to the royals and believe the rules that apply to the wider world do not apply to them, and since they can say and do as they please because their livelihoods are never at stake, their lives are very much like those lived by Edward VII, Alice Keppel and their friends a century and more ago.

Mocked by the media as a world of Tims who are nice but Dim, the English upper classes, though diminished in number, were until recently supported on their landed estates by vast subsidies – effectively state handouts – from the European Union. These largely made up for incomes lost to taxes and death duties in the early twenti-eth century – taxes that were fiercely resisted by the then Prince of Wales and his circle.

Charles and Camilla received these subsidies (and despite the recent Brexit vote will continue to receive them for some time) even though they are enormously wealthy anyway. Any concerns they may have had about Britain's so-called loss of sovereignty in the EU were more than compensated for by these state handouts. They helped ensure that Charles did not have to befriend financiers as his great-great-grandfather was forced to do; they helped instead to ensure that Charles and Camilla were and are able to live the opulent lives lived by both their ancestors. And as Alice Keppel, the subject of this book, knew: 'Love is all very well, but money is better.'

Introduction

OOKS ABOUT EDWARD VII and his circle return again and again to the same sources. These typically include papers held by the British royal family and other European royal families along with documents held in official or government archives. Many of these books make a point of thanking the royal family for allowing access to various official papers and this is almost certainly a sign that these books will have little genuinely new to tell us. This applies particularly to books about Queen Victoria and her son Edward VII because so much has deliberately been destroyed – what's left can be seen because it is usually innocuous.

Edward VII's life was so scandalous – numerous mistresses and perhaps half a dozen illegitimate children – that we can be sure the royal family has done as much as possible to conceal or destroy the most incriminating evidence. We know, for example, that Edward VII himself insisted all his personal papers and letters be destroyed after his death. This was, no doubt, partly due to the fact that the papers included painful memories recorded during his extremely unhappy childhood. But mostly the document bonfires that lasted for several days after the King died were part of a comprehensive effort to protect his reputation.

Alice Keppel became the Prince of Wales's mistress in 1898 and she remained his favourite mistress from then until his death in 1910. Alice got into bed with Bertie, as Edward was known to his friends, at the first opportunity because she wanted money and he had vast amounts of it. But Bertie was by no means the first wealthy man Alice had slept with for money. Almost from the day she married the Hon. George Keppel in 1891 she knew that she wanted to live among the very richest in the country and as her husband did not have the kind of money she needed, she was determined to get it by the only means open to her: the sale of her body to much wealthier men than her husband.

What makes the story particularly shocking is that Alice's husband was only too happy to live on the money Alice earned by sleeping with the King, various aristocrats and numerous bank managers.

Alice and George had two children, but, as this book will show, neither was fathered by Alice's husband. Both children were illegitimate and one, Sonia, is the grandmother of the present Duchess of

Cornwall, the former Camilla Parker Bowles, now wife of Charles, Prince of Wales. It is very possible – and indeed believed by many – that Sonia was fathered by Edward VII, Charles's own great-great-grandfather. This would make the Duchess of Cornwall a blood relation of her husband, albeit distantly.

Alice Keppel's affair with the Prince of Wales, later Edward VII, damaged the King's relationship with Queen Alexandra; Alice Keppel's great-granddaughter Camilla Parker Bowles's adulterous relationship with Prince Charles destroyed his relationship with his wife, the late Diana, Princess of Wales.

It was always said that Sonia Keppel was the daughter of Alice and George Keppel. By contrast it was a barely concealed secret that Sonia's elder sister Violet, born six years earlier than Sonia in 1894, was certainly not George Keppel's daughter. Violet's father was the MP and banker Ernest William Beckett (1856–1917), later Baron Grimthorpe, with whom Alice Keppel had an affair – in return for money – very soon after marrying the financially inadequate George Keppel.

Violet Keppel was to become notorious for a string of lesbian affairs in the 1920s and beyond, and her parentage became a matter of public speculation as a result. She was well known across fashionable London during her affair with Vita Sackville-West – an affair described in painful detail by West's son Nigel Nicolson in his book *Portrait of a Marriage*.

Alice's second daughter Sonia, by contrast, stayed out of the public eye, partly because she was far more conventional than her sister but also to avoid drawing attention to her dysfunctional family and the very real possibility that she might in fact be the daughter of King Edward VII.

The destruction of Edward VII's private papers was carried out in accordance with the King's wishes by his private secretary Francis Knollys. Edward's long-suffering wife, Queen Alexandra, also insisted on her death that all her papers should be destroyed, and for similar reasons. In Alexandra's case Charlotte Knollys, Francis's wife, burnt the papers.

Had the Knollys's servants behaved as Edward had behaved, the couple would have thrown them out on the street, but the rules were different for a King and Queen – however messy their lives, their reputations must be protected. That at least was, and is, the view of the royal family and their immediate circle.

Embarrassing documents that escaped the fires and might have turned up in succeeding years were also destroyed by a notoriously secretive family understandably embarrassed by the antics of a King who spent most of his life chasing other men's wives and, when necessary, either bending the law or breaking it to avoid any repercussions for himself.

Edward's most significant extramarital affair was with Alice Keppel, and this book is the story of her life. I have drawn to a limited extent on published versions of her life as well as official papers and the memoirs of those who knew her and the people around her. I say to a limited extent because memoirs of the time were mostly written by people who shared, to a large extent, Alice's values and aristocratic background and they therefore had every reason to hide the truth about her. Osbert Sitwell, for example, describes her charm and humour; Princess Alice writes almost as if Alice Keppel were Mother Teresa of Calcutta. Virginia Woolf, a rebel from Victorian and Edwardian values of hypocrisy and deceit, was one of the few to write bluntly about Mrs Keppel. After meeting her at lunch in 1932 Woolf wrote:

> I lunched with Raymond [Mortimer] to meet Mrs Keppel; a swarthy, thick set, raddled, direct ('My dear' she calls one) old grasper: whose fists have been in the money bags these 50 years: but with boldness: told us how her friends used to steal, in country houses in the time of Ed. 7th. One woman purloined any jewelled bag left lying. And she has a flat in the Ritz; old furniture; &c. I liked her on the surface. I mean the extensive, jolly, brazen surface of the old courtesan; who has lost all bloom; & acquired a kind of cordiality, humour, direct-ness instead. No sensibilities as far as I could see; nor snobberies; immense superficial knowledge, & going off to Berlin to hear Hitler speak. Shabby underdress: magnificent furs: great pearls: a Rolls Royce waiting – going off to visit my old friend the tailor; and so on.

The anglophile American novelist Henry James called Bertie 'Edward the Caresser' and he thought his character and relationship with Alice Keppel 'quite particularly vulgar'.

But we must weigh against this the many statements that recall Alice Keppel's good qualities – her kindness, for example, at least to her social equals. Harold Acton, famously a member of the Brideshead set at Oxford in the 1920s, later lived in Italy close to where Alice Keppel had her final home. He said of her: 'She possessed enormous charm, which was not only due to her cleverness and vivacity, but to her generous heart.'

Alice was also the last word in discretion and secrecy; she was, if anything, more secretive even than the royal family. She left no significant papers, and would have been horrified at the idea of writing her memoirs. When in later life she heard of the scandal surrounding Edward and Mrs Simpson, she famously remarked that things had been better done in her day – meaning affairs and sleeping with men for money were fine so long as no one found out or made a fuss if they did. When in 1921 Alice heard that Daisy Brooke, another of Edward VII's former mistresses, planned to write her memoirs, Alice condemned the idea as a breach of a 'sacred' relationship.

<hr>

I had long wanted to write about Alice Keppel's life, but it was only in the early 1980s while researching a book on domestic servants that, quite by chance, I met and interviewed at great length a remarkable woman who, from her early teens, had worked as a maid for the Keppels.

Agnes Florence Cook, known to her friends as Flo, was a mine of information about the Keppel household from the late 1890s until

1924 when the Keppels effectively left England for good. Many of Agnes's tales came down to her from her mother and grandmother, who had also worked for the Keppels. Agnes, who was in her late eighties when I met her, had a remarkably detailed memory of life in the Keppel's grand London houses seventy and more years earlier, and it is these memories that inform much of this book.

The story Agnes told me was deeply shocking in many ways, revealing as it did that Alice Keppel was prepared to sleep with almost anyone rich enough to make it worth her while and that Camilla Duchess of Cornwall's grandmother may well have been fathered by Prince Charles's own great-great-grandfather.

The convention that describes upper-class women who sleep with men for money as 'mistresses' seemed to Agnes entirely unfair. A woman from what used to be called the lower orders would always be referred to as a prostitute or a kept woman if she slept with men for money so why did the same or similar labels not attach to more aristocratic women living similar lives? According to Agnes it was another example of one rule for the rich and another for the poor.

Agnes's memories stayed with her for decades because she felt deeply the injustices of a world where servants were seen as scarcely human. They were expected to devote their lives to the families for whom they worked and for little financial reward. Agnes herself spent more than a decade working fourteen-hour days in the Keppel household for very little money and with only one afternoon off each week. Even this free time was strictly controlled by the family. Talking to servants from other houses was strictly forbidden; boyfriends were strictly forbidden.

Grand houses were built with separate servants' staircases so the family might have as little contact with the people who looked after them as possible. If by chance Agnes or one of the other lower servants met a member of the family on the main stairs she was instructed to turn to face the wall. Any servant who forgot to do this and made eye contact with a member of the family faced instant dismissal. It was all a far cry from the absurd fiction of television's *Downton Abbey*.

Rose Plummer, a friend of Agnes who also worked as a maid in many great London houses in the 1920s, recalled the kind of thing servants had to put up with:

> I was on the landing at the right time – that is, when the family should have been elsewhere – dusting away when I heard someone coming up the main stairs. I didn't have time to dodge into a bedroom or down the back stairs, which is what you were supposed to do, so I just turned to face the wall and, bearing in mind what had happened before when I'd got told off for glancing up, I made sure I kept my eyes on the little flowers on the wallpaper.
>
> Next thing was I felt him stop behind me. He just stopped and I thought, 'Bloody hell. He's got stuck. Or he thinks I shouldn't be here.'
>
> A bit of me wanted to giggle. Then I froze. I felt a hand on my bum. It wasn't just a light pat. He left his hand there quite gently for a bit then pushed and tried to get his fingers right between my legs.
>
> I had my big apron on and my dress as well as thick stockings – with very attractive thick pads sewn to the knees! – and a giant pair of bloomers made out of cotton as thick as sailcloth, so I knew he

wasn't going to get very far. But I wasn't really shocked. I didn't think of it as a sexual assault while it was happening. I didn't think of anything. I was just surprised by what seemed to be happening.

I think he was disappointed and having shoved a bit more and done some odd noisy breathing he stopped and I heard him go off down the corridor.

This was the grubby underpinning of an aristocratic – and royal – world that wanted society to think it represented the height of moral probity.

✻—❀❀—✻

There has never been a full biography of Alice Keppel despite the fact that she is one of the most fascinating figures of late nineteenth- and early twentieth-century British history, a figure who personifies the late Victorian and Edwardian era of upper-class decadence and vast social inequality.

Most of the published material refers to Mrs Keppel as the King's confidante or his *maîtress en titre*, or as 'la favourite'. The suggestion is that her position in relation to Edward had a semi-official air about it; that her role was far more than that of sexual partner. It's as if historians and biographers have been seduced by Alice just as Edward VII was. Biographies of the King all repeat the same clichés about Alice. They emphasise how good she was for Bertie – she kept him in a good temper, she was a conduit for various powerful figures who wished to influence the King, she knew how to soothe and flatter him, she knew how to keep him in temper as no one else could. She is therefore seen in almost every history of the period as a benign influence; as someone who enabled Edward VII to be much better (and better-tempered) than he might otherwise have been.

Royal biographers who trot out the same old stories about Alice's virtues and good influence on the King tend to forget that flattering and soothing him arguably made him more unreasonable, more difficult to deal with, not less. And the effect of Alice's constant presence on Queen Alexandra tends to be played down, and little mention is made of the fact that Mrs Keppel was the first to sack any of her servants who she believed to be behaving immorally, even if that 'immorality' amounted to no more than having a boyfriend or 'follower', to use the jargon of the time.

Alice Keppel always did as she pleased so long as the outward show of respectability was maintained. Her life was underpinned by attitudes that were to destroy her daughter Violet's chance of happiness, and two generations on, those same attitudes caused the divorce of the present Prince of Wales from his first wife.

Alice could sleep around but the servants could not – this hypocrisy is something Agnes Cook never forgot. The upper-class attitude to servants can perhaps best be seen in Nigel Nicolson's embarrassed description of his mother Vita Sackville-West stepping over a servant scrubbing the front step of a grand London house as if the poor woman was simply a parcel.

The real life of Alice Keppel lies behind the official versions trotted out by biographers and historians who often suffer from a perhaps unconscious tendency to treat the upper classes with a level of deference they would not afford lesser mortals.

This unacknowledged bias also afflicts those who write about Bertie, as Prince of Wales and later as Edward VII. Certainly his philandering is mentioned and often at length, but the emphasis is always on the fact that despite his womanising, his gross overeating and his almost pathological love of pleasure, he managed to get some work done. Official histories somehow become squeamish at the idea that he was a selfish, idle, bad-tempered, immature man who lost his temper if the whole world did not dance attendance on him. Friends' wives were expected to sleep with him automatically; aristocratic women such as Mrs Keppel and others were expected to become his mistresses. No one was ever allowed to complain at how they were treated.

Can we really believe that so many women would have slept with this 5ft 7in. man with a 48in. waist who stank of cigars and sweat if he had not been King? The emphasis on his kingly qualities is absurd. He could speak French and German, it is true, and he liked to keep up his continental connections – largely because brothels and gambling were legal in France while they were illegal in Britain – but there was little to his statesmanship beyond that.

The writer A. N. Wilson makes the point that Edward's diplomatic skills lay not in his abilities but in the fact that he let professional politicians get on with it rather than, like his mother, constantly interfering in areas where he could contribute nothing. It is true that Edward, though quick to anger, could be charming and was often at pains to put lesser mortals at their ease, but as one of his friends commented, 'he was happy to ignore his own rank so long as no one else did'.

❋─❋❋─❋

This book starts from the premise that Edward VII really couldn't be bothered much with work if he could possibly avoid it. His childhood, as we will see, destroyed any interest he might have had in anything beyond enjoying himself in brothels, gambling dens and in the beds of other men's wives. His bleak early years produced an adult who expected Parliament to provide him with millions of pounds each year (in today's values) so he could lead a playboy life of tantrums and over-indulgence, hypocrisy and cruelty. He was good to his favourites, but liked occasionally to humiliate them as he did regularly with his friend and fellow rake Sir Christopher Sykes.

An anonymous critic writing in *The Clarion* in the 1880s implied that Bertie's mother Queen Victoria would not have had the brains to become a maid if she had not been lucky enough to be born a Princess. Her son was perhaps little better, but then the sort of childhood experiences he endured were never going to produce a well-balanced adult.

❋─❋❋─❋

Charles I lost his head because he would not accept that the days when monarchs had absolute political power were over. His son

Charles II was wiser and therefore devoted his life to pleasure not power, knowing that he could still use his position to ennoble his friends and illegitimate children and make them rich, and to seduce any woman who took his fancy. Bertie was remarkably similar. It's as if power must find an outlet; monarchs without political power inevitably enjoy wielding personal power.

My main sources for this book are not, as I have said, the usual official histories, nor have I had access to the Keppel family papers, nor indeed to the royal archives. What would be the point? That has all been done before.

The destruction of Edward and Alexandra's papers may have been a tragedy for historians but the act of destruction itself speaks volumes. There is no doubt Bertie's letters would have revealed a string of mistresses and casual affairs – including affairs with what were then known as common prostitutes. They would also have revealed that the King interfered on several occasions with the justice system and was utterly ruthless in his treatment of anyone who threatened to expose him. He was supported in this by numerous aristocratic members of the establishment who would have been the first to condemn such behaviour in lesser mortals.

The dark side of Bertie's life, the side that went up in flames with his papers, can at last be glimpsed through the memories of someone who was there. Someone who lived in the Keppels' house when Bertie visited, as he did regularly, to have tea and sex with Alice Keppel while her husband was away from home. And Agnes Cook's memories don't just relate to life in the Keppel household. They reveal a network of communication between numerous servants working at the Keppel's various houses over the decades, for despite their employers' best efforts to prevent their servants gossiping, gossip they did. They managed to communicate with each other, and Agnes's mother's servant grapevine included friends below stairs at Bertie's London home Marlborough House, at Buckingham Palace, Sandringham and the Keppels' family houses in Norfolk and in Scotland.

The long silence of those destroyed royal papers can now be broken and through Agnes Cook's first-hand, often eyewitness accounts of those far-off days we get a remarkable glimpse of the real world of Alice and Bertie: a world with no moral compass; a world of hypocrisy and deceit, of criminality and illegitimacy and all in the name of pleasure and money.

Chapter 1

Alice – 'Not Quite Top Drawer'

ALICE FREDERICA EDMONSTONE came from a family that was always a little too keen to emphasise its ancient lineage and its royal connections. Her male ancestors were almost invariably military men who were often also given ceremonial posts at court that amounted to little more than sinecures. The earliest record of the family appears to be that of Henricus

I

de Edmoundiston who lived near Edinburgh in the mid-thirteenth century. But the family really sprang from Culloden near Inverness. Here, Duntreath Castle in Strathblane had been given to William Edmonstone by Robert III in the mid-fourteenth century. Edmonstone had married Robert's daughter Mary, and the castle was a wedding present. This royal connection, however ancient, was one the Edmonstones were always keen to recall.

But by the mid-nineteenth century the family was indistinguishable from any English aristocratic family. After the destruction of Catholic claims to the throne the Scottish aristocracy fell over each other in their haste to seem more English than the English. Their male children were schooled at Eton and Harrow and it was the ultimate disgrace for a member of a family such as the Edmonstones to speak with a Scottish accent.

Alice's family looked to London and spoke in patrician tones that would sound absurdly clipped by today's standards, and via marriage for the daughters and commissions in the army for the sons, they expected preferment and lucrative employment as of right.

Many of Alice Edmonstone's seventeenth- and eighteenth-century ancestors had also been lawyers and MPs. Sir William Edmonstone, Alice's father, was born at Hampton in Middlesex, now part of greater London, in 1810. He joined the navy as a young man, served in India and had risen to the rank of rear admiral by 1869 and then full admiral in 1880. From 1874–1880 he was also MP for Stirlingshire.

William married Alice's mother, Mary Elizabeth Parsons, in 1841. She was the daughter of the British resident of the Greek island of Zakynthos. He was effectively governor of the Ionian islands.

In addition to Duntreath Castle, a vast pile largely rebuilt in the nineteenth century, the Edmonstones had a house in Edinburgh and rented a house each year in London's Belgravia, but they were not rich by the standards of the aristocrats who dominated London society.

Edward VII was to be the centre of this world and he enjoyed an annual income of roughly £11 million (in today's values) while the Edmonstone estates produced around £200,000–£300,000 a year in today's values.

This made the family feel relatively poor, but one should remember a large suburban house on the outskirts of London in 1900 might cost around £1,000 to buy, so aristocratic expectations then as now were high. If landowners and the upper classes have a sense of entitlement today it is nothing to the sense of entitlement felt by the Edmonstones and others like them a century and more ago.

The expectation of preferment at court was a way to augment diminishing rents from land and relatively small amounts of army pay. And the Edmonstones might have been far poorer had they not been able gradually to sell off land to railway companies expanding across Scotland in the last decades of the nineteenth century. Earlier on the family had also sold their Irish estates to make ends meet.

The problem for William Edmonstone was that he had nine children – Alice, born in 1868, was the last – and expected them all to live as the Edmonstones had always lived. But the estates, or what remained of them, could not produce the money to keep the family in the style they felt was their due. The need for good marriages was therefore paramount, but there was a further difficulty. Eight of William Edmonstone's children were daughters who needed dowries. Had they been sons the situation would have been easier, but the old cultural norms still held sway and daughters were much more expensive to marry off well.

Of course other aristocratic families found themselves in the same position and looked for wealthy marriages for their children. This was why numerous American heiresses – more than seventy between 1880 and 1920 – were able to marry into the increasingly desperate British aristocracy. The aristocracy would have loved to continue to marry only within and across the families they had always married but taxes and the fall in land values made this impossible.

This chink in the armoury of the British class structure was spotted by status-obsessed Americans who had money but no history or titles, so they sent their daughters and sons to London to buy their way into the peerage. And it worked. It was a tradition that to some extent dated back to the eighteenth century – a tradition satirised by Hogarth in his series of paintings *Marriage à-la-mode*, where an aristocratic family allows a wealthy industrialist to marry into the family in return for money.

This was the background to Alice's childhood. The family was ancient and well connected but not quite rich and well connected enough. They were also Presbyterians who took a strict view of morality and the rules of behaviour – ironic, given Alice's future career. In later life Alice's sisters, who all married clergymen, soldiers or minor landowners, hated even to mention Alice and what they saw as her embarrassingly sordid life.

Agnes Cook recalled that when Alice occasionally visited one of her siblings she would joke about expecting a frosty welcome;

she rarely in fact visited any of them with the sole exception of her brother Archie, whom she adored and whose family she supported financially throughout his life. Archie would never have judged his sister since he benefited from her relationship with various wealthy men, especially Edward VII. Indeed, it was Alice who persuaded Edward VII to give Archie a well-paid job as groom-in-waiting in 1907. Needless to say, the job involved almost no work at all. But there is no doubt her other siblings wanted little to do with her. They would have shunned her completely, but as her illicit relationship was by then with the King, they had to stifle their protests.

This was all far in the future when Alice was born in 1868 at Duntreath Castle. Or is that where she was born? The biographers disagree, some insisting she was actually born not in Scotland, but at Woolwich at the naval dockyard where her father was superinten-dent, a role not unlike that of comptroller of the navy, a job held by Samuel Pepys more than two centuries earlier. Her father was nearly sixty when she was born and had not yet succeeded to the baron-etcy – which is why they may have been living at Woolwich rather than at Duntreath. Her mother, Mary Elizabeth, was twenty years younger than her husband, but still decidedly a geriatric mother by the standards of the time.

Alice was the prettiest girl in the family and her nickname was always Freddie after her middle name Frederica. Family legend has it that in her early years she was boisterous, argumentative and very much a tomboy who liked to get her own way. She was also decisive and rather masculine both in appearance and manner. By the time she reached her teens she realised that being a tomboy was frowned upon and she gave it up almost overnight, but her confidence and assurance remained. Her argumentative nature gave way slowly to a curious, steely will combined with charm and good looks; she quickly realised these were the qualities that would get her what she wanted without the need for loud protests. Her daughter Violet recalled her good humour and her lack of malice. Even when she was telling a funny story about someone the story never had a cruel edge. She had a reputation which she retained throughout her life of never being deliberately malicious.

Alice learned to be what we today would call manipulative. She could get people to do as she wished. One of her siblings said:

> Freddie suddenly stopped upsetting people with her rowdy behaviour and chose instead a subtle but very firm approach that involved never losing her temper but also never giving up till she had gained her object. She smiled but would brook no opposition and she had that rare skill which involves persuading other people that they want to do what you want them to do.

Life at Duntreath revolved around the unchanging pastimes of the rural aristocracy: riding, shooting and fishing, stalking, large family meals, and the whole edifice supported by numerous servants. Among the children only Alice and Archie seemed to take any interest in these pursuits. Indeed, Archie, who enjoyed painting throughout his life, was remarkably similar to George Keppel, the man Alice was later to marry. Archie disliked rough sports, was quiet, meticulous and unobtrusive. Having been brought up surrounded by girls this was perhaps hardly surprising, but he also deferred to Alice in everything and allowed her to take charge completely of his life as a child and as an adult.

Alice disliked lessons but loved playing outside and already enjoyed male conversation, whether that of her father, the footmen or the stable lads. Like all aristocratic children she was expected to be neither seen nor heard when she was very young, but she had an uncanny ability to charm her father, especially out of his occasional gloomy moods. Her sisters claimed that she manipulated him, but whatever the truth, she was certainly her father's favourite, and the rules that normally applied to Victorian girls were relaxed for her.

Governesses ran the nursery and the older children's lives and at most the younger children might expect to be presented to their parents once a day in the early evening, well dressed and carefully coached into saying something intelligent or amusing or both.

Well-born mothers of new infants still packed them off to a wet nurse as the idea that an aristocratic woman would breast-feed her own children was considered probably indecent and certainly disgusting. Queen Victoria herself loathed the whole idea of babies and small children, and in this as in so much else she set the tone for the upper classes of the nineteenth century.

Alice's great love as a child, and it was a love shared by her favourite sibling Archie, was gardening and flowers and for the rest of her life her various houses were always filled with blooms that she insisted were changed every day. At Duntreath as a child and later in life she and Archie would design and plant out new parts of the garden while the men set off for the hill to shoot stags.

According to family legend a bored twelve-year-old Alice set off one day with her brother Archie and climbed Ben Lomond. Her mother was horrified, feeling this was decidedly unladylike. But then Alice did not aspire to be like her mother, who seems to have been a vague presence obsessed with painting – a love she passed on to only one of her children, Archie.

Every summer the family left Scotland and lived in a rented house in London's Belgravia.

Agnes Cook recalled the gossip about young Alice among the servants:

> Well, the family came to London for what was called the season – girls coming out I mean and visiting all the families they knew. They were looking for suitable husbands even from when the girls were eight or ten and when I say suitable I mean from a very closed circle of families – just a few hundred families ran the whole of London society. Anyway my grandmother and mother told me all the servants used to be amazed that Alice was always playing with the boys while her sisters were much more serious but she had the family boldness and was really much more like a boy. She used to come down to the kitchen where she wasn't really supposed to come at all, my grandmother said, and ask if there were any cakes. Well there were always cakes or something and she'd have to be answered as if she was her ladyship. My grandmother said that if she fancied something she would just say 'give me that', take it and walk off without a word of thanks.
>
> Her sisters were all much older, more like aunts really and far more serious than Alice who had almost nothing to do with them then or

thereafter. Her sister Mary married the Lord Advocate of Scotland, another married a major and a third a vicar. They were all worthy but very boring. Alice felt she had little or nothing in common with them. She was determined I think to have a more exciting life; to do better and she had the looks to do it. My grandmother said she was glorious-looking as a young girl.

Mind you, she was still very attractive when I knew her later on. Rumours had it that she used to kiss the stable lads when she was a girl just to see what it was like but I think that was probably said because of how she later behaved – you know, sleeping with the King and all sorts of men who used to come to the house when her husband was away.

By the time she was in her teens Alice's sisters had all married and left to live in various places across Scotland. That sort of provincial life would never do for the precocious and already ambitious Alice, who longed to be in London and escape the long dreary days in the Highlands.

Like most aristocratic girls in the second half of the nineteenth century Alice received no formal education at all. She read to Archie and he read to her and like all well-born girls she learned to dance and especially enjoyed Scottish reels. She was by all accounts an accomplished dancer, which no doubt stood her in good stead when she visited Balmoral years later with the King.

There was a widespread idea among the upper classes that well-born men disliked well-educated girls, which is why they were excluded from English public schools and from the old universities. Even when they were finally admitted to Oxford and Cambridge they could not be awarded degrees. Cambridge, for example, only began awarding women degrees after the end of the Second World War. But even the social accomplishments typically expected of a girl of Alice's class appear to have been largely missing – Alice never spoke French well, unlike her daughter Violet who was a brilliant linguist, and she did not play the piano or paint. But an upbringing that involved learning very little was in some ways considered the correct upbringing for a girl who was expected to marry someone with a title and rich enough to ensure she could spend the rest of her life simply organising lunches and dinner parties.

A life of conspicuous leisure was the highest aspiration for the upper classes and aristocracy. To have to work was the ultimate disgrace and this was a lesson Alice learned early. If marriage brought the chance to do nothing but eat, drink and socialise, it also brought the chance to be free. Marriage was the ultimate sign that a girl had arrived, and she then became a central part of the favourite sport of a significant portion of the idle rich: adultery. Many aristocratic men were so bored by the lack of anything serious to do that they spent their lives trying and often succeeding in sleeping with each other's wives – it was a pastime rather like shooting, in which the idea was to bag as many birds as possible. Married women were fair game because, as Lord Alington (later one of Alice's lovers) put it, 'they had been broken in'. Unmarried daughters were very different and only a cad of the lowest type would try to seduce a friend's unmarried sisters. The rule was that if you took a fancy to a young girl you waited till she had married and then seduced her. Daughters were carefully chaperoned until marriage after which – bizarrely – they could sleep with whomever they liked so long as they were discreet about it. Of course there were many exceptions to this, but where it occurred it was considered bad form to make a fuss and beyond the pale to resolve the issue in the divorce courts.

In their remote castle at Duntreath and in their rented London house in Belgravia, marriage was the future state that all the Edmonstone children, but especially the girls, would have aspired to; the terror for women was to be left on the shelf, but marriage was also important for sons, who had a dynastic duty to produce children of their own after marrying rich heiresses. For Alice there was an additional incentive – her habit of kissing the stable lads while she played with them at Duntreath as a girl was not entirely innocent. It is a reminder that Alice was highly sexed. Agnes Cook recalled Alice during her long affair with Edward VII:

Among the servants the gossip was that the King, Edward VII I mean, was often dragged back into Alice's private apartments when he was trying to leave, which was always around half past four or five o'clock in the afternoon. Alice, laughing, would say, 'Perhaps just once more,' and pull him back in a playful way. They both used other phrases that we servants thought were disgusting but then we were far more prudish than they were. Anyway, the King got very excited when she suggested he stay with her a little longer and they would then disappear again into her private rooms. One of the maids was always complaining about the disgusting state of the sofa after Edward had been to the house and I don't think she was talking about cigar ash, although there was also a lot of that!

Duntreath was always a place Alice was happy to return to, partly because it held memories of her father who died when she was still in her teens and with whom she had a very close relationship. She was more ambivalent about her mother, who seems to have dreamed her life away. Alice loathed her mother's passivity and much preferred her father's forcefulness, so it is no wonder she modelled herself on him. Her curious blend of feminine charm and masculine determination were noted by friends and family throughout her life.

Despite her early years rushing about the estate playing with the stable lads, by her late teens Alice was hugely conscious of her charms and she spent a great deal of time – as she was to do for the rest of her life – dressing very carefully to emphasise her striking looks. She knew that her aristocratic background and her beauty were assets that would enable her to escape the confines of family life. She also knew that with the right kind of marriage she would be able to take Archie with her and look after him for the rest of his life.

By the age of eighteen Alice was well known in London society among the few hundred families who mattered and also happened to have eligible sons. This was hardly surprising since everyone in society knew everyone else, and mothers and grandmothers, aunts and godmothers spent their lives matchmaking and considering various marriage options for daughters, granddaughters and nieces.

The death of Alice's father in 1888 would have spurred Alice's desire to marry and escape the restrictions of home life. Her future husband, George Keppel, whom she first met around this time, had many of the attributes of her father. Like the old admiral, George was affable, easy-going, often vaguely absent – qualities that Archie also possessed and which seemed always to attract Alice because they allowed her to take the dominant role.

The servants in the London house the family rented for the season when Alice was nineteen recalled that she flirted outrageously with all the young men she met – so much so she was known as 'flirtatious Freddie', and it was not entirely a term of approbation. When she was younger even her mild-mannered father suggested to her that it was unseemly behaviour and, shocked, for a while she behaved far more self-consciously, but her true nature could not be denied and she was soon meeting men whenever and wherever she could. The golden rule that unmarried society women were never seduced protected her, but it also prevented her satisfying what the biographer Raymond Lamont-Brown called her 'raging need for sexual congress'.

By the late 1880s the influence of the aesthetes and of Oscar Wilde in particular was beginning to be felt, and flamboyant colours and cynical jokes – especially in plays such as *The Importance of Being Earnest* – were disturbing the dull colours and morbid seriousness Queen Victoria, in her perpetual mourning, had made fashionable. The old ways were being adapted and occasionally discarded. Elderly female relatives deplored, for example, the new practice of eating in public restaurants. It was considered fast and dangerous.

Restaurants were for the middle classes – the 'bedints', as the upper classes called them. The aristocracy ate in each other's houses, served by footmen, and were disgusted by the idea of eating in public. It was unseemly, but times were changing.

The railways, like the new restaurants, had been blamed by an older generation for what they saw as increasing immorality; certainly it is true that the railway made it easier for the smart set to enjoy Friday to Monday breaks at each other's houses and it was here that bedroom-hopping was all the rage. The railway and the ease and speed of travel it allowed were to be central to the love life of that master of adultery – Edward VII.

Like many young people Alice loved whatever was exciting and new and when she was offered the chance to eat in the newly fashionable restaurants she took it. She was living what Queen Victoria would have denigrated as a 'fast' life, but aged nineteen and with her father dead and her quiet brother Archie as her only chaperone she was able to enjoy far more freedom than other aristocratic girls her age. She even took up smoking and was an avid cigarette smoker for the rest of her life. It was in a restaurant, probably Romano's in London's West End, that she first met her future husband George Keppel.

Chapter 2

George – The Man Who Wasn't There

T HE KEPPELS HAD far more scandals in their history than the Edmonstones, but they were perceived as being slightly higher up the aristocratic ladder, which no doubt added to the appeal for Alice. She would have assumed that a loftier position on the social scale must mean more money. Discovering that this was not in fact the case was to be a tremendous shock. It made her realise that one could take nothing for granted and that romantic relationships are all very well but they must also be lucrative.

The greatest Keppel scandal did not involve money, or at least not directly; it involved homosexuality at a time when the penalty for gay relationships was death. The Keppel who founded the English branch of the family was Arnold Joost van Keppel (1670–1718) who arrived in England with the Dutch King William. The young man was known teasingly as a court beauty (a term usually used of women) and he was given the earldom of Albemarle by William III in 1697, largely because William wanted to sleep with Arnold and almost certainly did sleep with him. It is difficult to believe the young man, who had nothing to commend him but his looks, would have been ennobled for less. From then on the van Keppels seem to have found regular employment, generation after generation, in the royal bedchambers (if not the royal beds) of succeeding monarchs. It was this link that gave the Keppels the edge over the Edmonstones.

Like most English aristocrats the Keppels also played at being soldiers, and expected (and were usually given) titles and positions at court – positions such as gentlemen of the bedchamber or aide de camp, both jobs that involved little more than hanging around waiting to be asked to pass writing paper or lavatory paper to the King. They were what we might today call hangers-on – friends of the royal family who hoped to benefit financially from the association.

The first Keppel is a case in point. In addition to the earldom of Albemarle, Arnold received the enormous sum of 200,000 guilders in William III's will.

Selling sex for favours and cash was to become Alice Keppel's forte, but before then there was at least one other sexual scandal in the Keppel family. While sailing to South Africa in 1860, rear admiral Sir Henry Keppel had started an affair with fellow passenger Lucy, Lady Grey. As he was on active service this was a serious dereliction of duty. Sir Henry was travelling to South Africa to take command of the British Navy there. A furious Lord Grey ensured that the scandal reached the British newspapers, but Grey forgot one vital fact – Henry Keppel was one of the Prince of Wales's best friends, a constant presence at the Prince's side at Cowes, at various brothels, at gambling dens and at the races.

The Prince used his influence to ensure that Sir Henry Keppel was not dismissed or even demoted as others undoubtedly would have been. Instead, he was promoted to Admiral of the Fleet – such was the power of royal patronage. This was one of Alice Keppel's favourite stories and it was one from which she learned a simple lesson: social prestige and position all stem from royal patronage. It was a lesson she never forgot.

❊·❊❊·❊

George Keppel was born in 1865. He was the fifth of the nine children of William Coutts Keppel, the seventh Earl of Albemarle, and his wife Sophia. Like many fashionable aristocrats at the time, William Coutts Keppel, under the influence of Cardinal Newman and the Oxford Movement, had converted to Catholicism, but religion was to play little part in his son George's life. With two elder brothers including Arnold, the heir to the title, George knew from his earliest days that he would have to make his own way in the world.

The Keppel family estates had been in decline for many years, largely because the family spent money like aristocrats but without much regard as to where the money might come from. Over time they were forced to sell land and property to keep themselves in the style they felt was their due. It was said that the family home, Quidenham Hall near Attleborough in Norfolk, had gradually lost all of its mahogany doors, marble statues, carvings, furniture and best pictures to pay the debts of a mad ancestor. Madness or at least eccentricity certainly ran in the family – Charlotte Susannah, wife of the fourth Earl, was known as the 'rowdy dowager' because wherever she went she shouted at people and threw things at them.

It was at Quidenham that George grew up and, like many children with numerous siblings, he seems to have received very little parenting, being passed between nannies and governesses until he was old enough to go to school. It was an upbringing that made him retreat into himself. He was easy-going it is true, but he rarely let anyone know what he really felt about anything. As Alice's brother Archie half-jokingly once said, 'When George comes into a room it's as if no one is there.'

George seems to have shown an interest in very little other than being exceptionally tidy and obsessed with his appearance. He shot pheasants occasionally, and played bridge, but mostly enjoyed tidying his rooms. He had no academic interests at all but at over six feet, well built and with a long twirling moustache, he was considered handsome. As an adult he spent hours each day dressing with the help of his valet. He used a tiny pair of silver tongs to curl his long waxed moustache. He changed his clothes several times a day throughout his life and it was said, only partly in jest, that this was his sole occupation. It was also said that he looked like a stage villain from a Victorian melodrama, but he behaved like a perfect gentleman and somehow seemed, as the writer Rebecca West noted, more beautiful than his wife.

It was said that pretty soon after George married Alice he stopped sleeping with her, being unable to cope with the messiness of sharing his room and bed with another person. He disliked the idea of his wife's bodily functions. He was aloof, charming and easily pleased. As one friend remarked, George liked to be led to pleasant occupations but not to do the leading.

His daughter Violet, recalling family tales of her father, wrote that as a teenager he had been so tall and thin and dark that he was known at school as the wolf. His academic career was undistinguished, but like so many of the dim younger sons of the aristocracy he was able to use family connections to enter the Royal Military College at Sandhurst where he was reprimanded for being 'lacklustre'.

Agnes Cook remembered George in later life:

> He was the fussiest bugger you can imagine. All his money and time were spent titivating as we used to call it. Even with the help of his valet — we used to feel sorry for the poor man — it would take him

hours to dress and then he might decide something was out of place and start all over again. But he had no interests or hobbies beyond smoking and going over to Hyde Park occasionally late at night or to a very seedy hotel in Jermyn Street to pick up girls. He had a thing about young girls with large bosoms. Beyond taking great care of his appearance and driving what he called his cuties in his carriage he did nothing.

After Sandhurst in 1886 George bought a lieutenant's commission in the army – in his case the Gordon Highlanders. Military life for George seems to have involved little beyond spending long hours in the officers' mess and playing cards. After marrying Alice Edmonstone in 1891 George quickly resigned his commission to concentrate on his life as a man of leisure.

George needed money to lead the life of ease he wanted – after all it was the only life he had ever known and he had no intention of learning to live according to the dictates of more modest means – but he also had to marry within a narrow social range, and when he met Alice in Romano's, two things would have struck him. First her charm and beauty (which included a large bosom) and second her membership of the right set. True, she was not quite as grand as the Keppels – as the son of an Earl, George was entitled to be known as 'the Honourable' – but there was that ancient royal connection and, besides, Alice would have made it very clear by her behaviour that she was going to take charge of George's life. George was a drifter who just wanted enough money to dine at his club, shoot pheasants, drive round the park and generally enjoy a quiet but lavish life. With this in mind, Alice must have seemed heaven sent, and there was also the financial angle to consider – George would have assumed that on marriage he would get his hands on Alice's money.

Unfortunately, while George was relying on Alice to rescue him from financial difficulties, Alice was also assuming that she would be financially comfortable for life if she married George. He was, after all, the son of an Earl, and must therefore be rich.

When they married after a short engagement in 1891, Alice was twenty-two; George was three years older. The wedding took place not in Scotland but at St Paul's Church, Knightsbridge, just a few hundred yards from the house in West Halkin Street where the couple planned to live.

By modern standards the financial settlement they received was staggeringly generous. George received £5,000 in trust from an aunt; Alice was given £15,000 – equivalent to around £2 million in today's values.

Alice was deeply shocked that more money was not forthcoming, but by then it was too late. They were married and had to make the best of it, but she was not prepared to live like a 'dim landowning squire from Shropshire'. Her instinct would immediately have been to try to do something about it.

She would have known that close relatives of George's – including, as we have seen, Rear Admiral Sir Henry Keppel – were already working for the Prince of Wales at nearby Marlborough House and that Keppel family tradition was closely linked to the royals. With these connections Alice would have assumed that sooner or later they would be asked to dine with people who dined regularly with the Prince of Wales.

Alice and George's joint fortune of £20,000 was simply not going to be enough to allow them to lead the life that Alice was determined to lead – a life that demanded a large number of servants, trips abroad, jewels, and dresses by the best couturiers in Europe. George had to be made into a stepping stone to that golden future.

Chapter 3

Marriage à la Mode

AFTER THEIR MARRIAGE, George and Alice moved into their new home. West Halkin Street was elegant but relatively small, and they soon moved to something bigger at nearby Wilton Crescent, a curving street of tall, late-Georgian terraced houses just off Belgrave Square. It was still a small house compared to nearby mansions, but perfectly situated in a fashionable district and close enough to Mayfair and the Prince of Wales's base at Marlborough House to ensure the couple would be on the radar.

The Keppels would have quickly received numerous invitations to the houses of other aristocratic families in London, many of whom they were already connected to by marriage. There is no doubt they were a dashing couple. With perfectly symmetrical features, vibrant chestnut hair, piercing blue eyes and an impressive figure, Alice was strikingly handsome. George was equally handsome with his dark hair, very pale skin and impressive stature. To modern eyes he bears an uncanny resemblance to the late unloved Lord Lucan, who murdered the family nanny.

Sometime in 1893 Alice became pregnant, but nobody ever believed that this child was George's. Hard pressed for cash already as they tried to keep up with the super-rich, Alice had taken matters into her own hands within months of her marriage. At a dinner party in Mayfair in 1891 – the same year in which she married George – she met the fabulously wealthy and recently widowed Ernest Beckett, whose family firm Beckett & Company provided loans and financial advice to the very rich. Ernest Beckett, though slightly looked down on for making his money from banking rather than land, was also the MP for Whitby and was soon to inherit the title Earl Grimthorpe.

According to servants' gossip recalled by Agnes Cook, Alice had slept with Beckett within a few weeks of meeting him:

My mother told me that Beckett was probably Mrs Keppel's first lover as she didn't have time to squeeze another one in in the few months between her marrying George Keppel and meeting Ernest Beckett. As a married woman she could visit Beckett at his house but he also came to Wilton Crescent. My mother said that even those servants who hadn't been around at the time of the Beckett affair knew about it and it was talked about for years afterwards because Beckett and Alice would almost rush to her private rooms when he arrived at the house. And the noise of them having sex was clearly audible to the butler who used to come down to the servants' hall and say to everyone, 'They're at it again.' Apparently the maids hated clearing up after Beckett had been and maybe Alice was even a bit embarrassed by what was going on as, after a while, most of their meetings took place at Beckett's house. But none of the servants doubted for a minute that Alice was determined to get Beckett into bed, not because he was a charmer or particularly good-looking – he was a bit of a bulldog in fact – but because she wanted his money.

Wherever it came from, money began to arrive in the Keppel coffers and in very large quantities.

Certainly around the time Violet Keppel was conceived, Alice and George were able to move from their house in Wilton Crescent to a far bigger Georgian house less than a mile directly north of Marlborough House. Number 30 Portman Square, built by the great architect James Wyatt (1746–1813), was designed on a grand scale, though not of course as grand as Marlborough House, where the Prince of Wales had his base. But it was certainly big enough for the dinner parties Alice had planned, parties to which the great and the good were to be invited over the coming years.

Since Alice was now earning money from Beckett it was natural that she should control the family expenditure. But Ernest Beckett was not only giving her money – he was also helping her with her own investments.

That Alice was being helped out of what she saw as her financial difficulties in return for sex was a barely concealed secret both above and below stairs. The servants all understood that George had agreed with Alice – it was an 'unholy pact', as Agnes Cook put it – that the only way they could hope to live in the style in which they wanted to live was for Alice to make money by sleeping with men who would be willing to pay for the privilege. In the coded language of the time, Alice was very good at making rich men happy. She clearly made Beckett happy and he continued to visit her regularly for a number of years whenever George was conveniently away, as Agnes Cook recalled:

> The servants at Portman Square knew what was going on – of course they did. The Keppels were definitely living above their means and, according to my mother, Ernest Beckett was definitely funding the whole thing. He looked like a dog on heat – that was the phrase the footman used when he described Beckett's arrival each week. He always came in the afternoon for tea, but the servants heard all sorts coming from the drawing room where she entertained him alone. George Keppel was always at his club at these times. I think they agreed it between them. They weren't sleeping together at this time – in fact some of the older servants thought that George had never ever slept with Alice. They thought it was a marriage of convenience. Certainly George and Alice had separate rooms all their lives. They would have breakfast at the same time late in the morning in their separate sets of rooms and

always in bed. It took George till lunchtime to get dressed – he was such a dandy – and then he would wander off to see his friends at his club where he secretly gambled, and Alice would prepare for her gentlemen visitors. And Beckett wasn't the only one. In fact, she started going to visit Beckett at his house after a few months so that he wouldn't bump into the other two men who used to call for tea in the afternoons at Portman Square. One of the other men was a very senior politician, or so the gossips said, and the other was a member of the House of Lords. The rule among the servants was that if Alice saw a man alone we were to stay well clear, because in those days you only saw a man alone in the afternoon for one thing and it wasn't a cup of tea!

Alice's drawing room had a sort of chaise longue in it and we called it the pouncing sofa. I don't think it was always the men who pounced either. John the footman used to say it was always Alice. She knew that if she once got a chap to have sex with her he was caught like a fly in a trap and would do anything for her afterwards. She never fell in love with these men – especially not Ernest Beckett who was a dull old thing – but she charmed them and entrapped them until they fell in love with her. Imagine you're just a dull old banker and a very pretty young married woman lunges at you, making it clear she'd like nothing more than for you to have sex with her. You'd soon give up all your money wouldn't you!

Family gossip suggests that Beckett gave Alice at least £5,000 during their affair and then took it back to invest for her in shares in the booming railways and other investments that produced fabulous dividends.

The case for Violet's true parentage also rests on the fact that, according to Agnes and her mother, George Keppel had stopped having sex with Alice within a few months of marrying her. There was a rumour that he may not even have consummated the marriage. Like many men he enjoyed the domestic sphere but it did not excite him sexually. He preferred women from a slightly lower social set and women married to his friends, but he would only meet them at their homes or at the houses of friends. He was far too fastidious about his own set of rooms at Portman Square to allow them to be disturbed by passionate embraces. A thoroughly modern man, he allowed his wife the same sexual freedoms he insisted on for himself. It was an open marriage very much of its time, a marriage not unlike, for example, the marriages of Vita Sackville-West and Harold Nicolson, or Earl and Countess Mountbatten or, in more recent times, Harold and Lady Macmillan. Like the Keppels, the Nicolsons and Macmillans stayed together, but the sexual aspects of their relationships were satisfied elsewhere.

When Violet Keppel was born in June 1894 she looked embarrassingly like Ernest Beckett and nothing at all like George Keppel, but George was delighted to have a child and didn't mind in the least that it could not possibly be his. Alice took a similar view. Children were an almost inevitable result of copulation and in those pre-DNA testing days, who could prove that a particular child had not been sired by a particular man? Besides, worrying about such things was no doubt seen as rather suburban. It was also rather suburban and definitely horribly middle class to consider children the central feature of a marriage. They were not. Society was all important and babies and children had nothing to contribute to that.

By the mid-1890s Alice and George were being invited to the grand houses of Belgravia and Mayfair and to the vast country houses of the landed aristocracy. They accepted invitations in 1895, for example, to the Earl of Derby's Knowsley Hall in Lancashire, to the Duke of Westminster's vast and gloomy Gothic pile near Chester and to Lord Alington's house at Crichel Down in Dorset.

The Keppels were expected to arrive with a vast array of luggage and their own servants. At home in London, champagne was expected to be served in almost unlimited amounts along with meals cooked by a French chef; Alice knew she must always entertain (and visit others) in her finest clothes, weighed down with jewels and furs. It was part of a system of signalling one's status to others. Alice had to look the part – anything else was unthinkable. Dress was everything and Alice was determined to out-dress everyone. She needed ropes of pearls and diamonds, she needed dresses from Worth in Paris. Her aim in life was to be noticed, especially by men. This cost a fortune but already that fortune was being made by the efforts of Beckett and the other wealthy men she had seduced. One's servants were also a vital part of the status game, as Agnes Cook remembered:

> Where we had made do with half a dozen servants in the Wilton Crescent house, we quickly went up to more than twenty in Portman Square. Having a large number of servants was almost the most

important sign of status then. People were impressed by lines of powdered footmen – their hair really was still powdered – and if it got
about that you only had a few maids and a housekeeper well you
would no longer be invited to the best houses. Having large numbers of servants was a sign of real importance.

The recently bereaved Ernest Beckett had no doubt been swept off
his feet by the brilliance and vivaciousness of a woman who, in the
words of the servants, wrapped bank managers and other wealthy
men around her little finger. Beckett would have been astonished
that this beautiful society woman should focus all her attention on
him. Certainly he would have known she was taking risks with her
reputation by driving with him in his carriage and visiting him regularly at his house in Piccadilly, but he was prepared to compensate
her for that risk.

In addition to regular large cheques, Beckett paid for Alice's
dresses from Worth in Paris, he bought her antiques from Duveen
in Bond Street and jewels from Asprey. But it was all done discreetly
as if these were simply gifts from a friend or an admirer.

Alice would have made no distinction between being in love
with a man and being in love with his money and in this sense she
was probably in love with Beckett. And if there was any doubt that
Violet was Beckett's child we should remember that Alice deliberately chose to name the child after Beckett's sister Violet. Agnes
Cook confirms the connection:

Everyone knew that Violet was Beckett's daughter – and according to my mother the servants just took it for granted. The servants' hall gossip was that Alice's husband didn't want to have sex with Alice – we thought he preferred boys! – so she had sex with people who could help her financially and also satisfy her craving for men. She really did adore men and I mean in the sexual sense – you could tell from the way she was with them, or at least that was what the butler said and he tended to let the men in and take them up to Alice's rooms and wait outside. The butler used to say that Alice was like a grand lady when she spoke to people or sat at the dinner table, but when her lovers arrived and sometimes there would be one or two others in addition to Beckett on the same day, she was like an animal once the bedroom door was closed.

You have to remember that servants lived in very close proximity to the people they worked for so they really knew what was going on. And very few employers even considered the possibility that the servants might notice anything. I know I've said it before but it does bear repeating – we were not seen as intelligent enough to understand what we saw and for those who did gossip there was always the threat of the sack. Some employers spoke French in front of the servants but neither George nor Alice spoke it well enough. Until the 1920s servants were also terrified of being sacked because without a good reference you couldn't get a new position. By the 1920s, and even more so the 1930s, servants were much harder to get because they'd escaped the tyranny of cap and apron (as we used to say) for better paid and less humiliating work in factories and shops. By 1930 some aristocratic old birds would take you if you had a criminal record because they were like babies. They had no idea how to do anything – they couldn't boil an egg because they'd never been taught. Alice Keppel was like that – she couldn't even wind her own watch.

Agnes recalled family gossip from an earlier generation:

My mother said that Alice Keppel was a bad woman but charming like the devil and ruthless to those who crossed her – which is why very few people ever dared to shun her for her behaviour later on with the King. She was also ruthless to those who gossiped about her but somehow servant gossip seemed to pass unnoticed. And some of the gossip was outrageous – I remember for example, my mother saying that the maids found strange devices in Alice's bedroom and soon gossip about them was all over the house. I think they were early condoms which Alice had bought probably on her trips to France.

As the 1890s wore on other names began to be whispered in the long list of Alice's wealthy conquests. While still sleeping with Beckett she was certainly conducting affairs with the Earl of Ilchester (Lord Stavordale) and with Baron Alington, whom she had seduced not at Crichel Down but at his London house just across Portman Square from the Keppels'.

There is no doubt that, once seduced, Stavordale and Alington would have been expected to be generous to the delightful Mrs Keppel. Giving her large sums of money now and then as well as expensive gifts would not have been seen as paying for sex but rather as aristocratic largesse in the game of adultery. And besides they could easily afford it and Alice was never one to decline a gift or fail to make it clear that in return for her sexual enthusiasm money was expected. And Alice had bills to pay. She had to keep her beloved brother Archie and his wife and new family as he had no intention of working to keep them. Alice also had to keep her husband George happy by buying him the finest clothes, jewellery and champagne, and she had to pay the large team of servants employed at Portman Square as well as the cost of a fine coach and horses and, later, expensive cars.

She always worried about money and towards the end of her life she became almost manically obsessed with having enough to continue to pay for things she felt were absolute necessities – her lady's maid, several housemaids, a cook, the butler and George's valet, governesses and nannies, gardeners and odd-job men. Alice was acutely aware of the role of sex and adultery as a means to make money and the highly charged sexual atmosphere at Portman Square that resulted had its influence below stairs, as Agnes Cook recalled:

The worst thing to be below stairs was a good-looking servant girl. Because they started very young, around twelve or thirteen in many cases, even working-class girls might look lovely for a bit until endless fifteen-hour days spent scrubbing floors and dishes made them old before their time. Well, the toffs who used to come to have sex with Mrs Keppel were always on the lookout for easier, younger prey and servant girls were always top of their list if they were good-looking.

The point was that no servant girl could say no to a lord, a gentleman as we used to say. She would almost certainly be sacked for insolence. Whoever was after her, whether Lord Alington or Stavordale or any of Mrs Keppel's other lovers, would use the threat of sacking as a lever to get what they wanted. Oddly it always seemed to be that the higher up the social scale these men were the worse they behaved. Earls were the worst because they thought they owned everyone. So any girl approached in this way had to give in and the best she'd hope for was five bob in return. She'd also just have to pray she wouldn't get pregnant or get a dose of the clap – most of the toffs in Mayfair and Belgravia had the clap because they were constantly having sex with anyone they could get hold of – boys, girls, the old women prostitutes in Hyde Park who sold oral sex once their charms had faded.

We had one very pretty maid who was just fourteen when she started at Portman Square. I'd started work at about the same age or a bit younger and so had my mother but we'd been warned what to expect. Nancy, poor thing, was a bit of an innocent, so when old Stavordale saw her crossing the hall and spoke to her we knew she was in trouble. One of Mrs Keppels' visitors had seduced Nancy within days and she was full of herself because he gave her a few trinkets. A month later she was in tears because he'd moved on to someone else. That was the way it was. George Keppel was the same. He didn't like sex with his wife but he enjoyed the company of any young girl with a big bosom. Anyway five months later Nancy was sacked when it was clear she was pregnant. Stavordale was probably the father but in those days if a girl got pregnant it was her fault. Disgusting really but that's how it was.

The increasing prosperity of the Keppels can be seen in their changing addresses. Their move from Wilton Crescent to Portman Square in 1899 would have been very expensive indeed and it is significant that this move became possible only after Alice began sleeping with the Prince of Wales; he provided her with enough money to live almost anywhere. It was the move to Portman Square that signalled Alice's elevated connections and entry into the world of the super-rich. Belgravia was smart and a cut above Kensington or Chelsea, but Alice would have known that it was not quite smart enough for the royal set at Marlborough House and it was Marlborough House on which she had set her sights.

It is difficult to say that Alice had designs on the Prince of Wales before she met him, but she had always known many people on the edge of his circle. Everyone expected that when the time came and she was formally introduced to him, she would exert all her charms to captivate. Why would she not? She had a habit of turning on her immense charm in exact proportion to the status and wealth of the person to whom she had been introduced.

In her memoirs her daughter Sonia noted how her mother had a very deliberate strategy when it came to meeting men. She would lift her veil carefully to increase the dramatic effect of uncovering her handsome face and she would address 'victims' (to use Agnes Cook's word) in a way that made them think every word they might utter was of the utmost interest. She made them feel they were the most important person in her universe. It was a trick that revealed she knew the strength of her charms. But once in her web there was no escape, unless Alice herself decided it was time to let someone go, and even then the letting go was so skilfully managed that former lovers almost always remained friends.

After Ernest Beckett's massive early boost to the Keppel finances there were other wealthy lovers happy to shower Alice with gifts and money, but her finances improved even more startlingly when she began to sleep with Humphrey Sturt, Lord Alington. Their affair had probably already been going on for some time when the Keppels moved to Portman Square. Conveniently, Alington had a house at 38 Portman Square just across the road from No. 30 where the Keppels moved in 1899. Alington was thereafter constantly at the Keppels' house – carefully fitted in around the Prince of Wales's visits – while George was conveniently out, usually at his club.

Servants' gossip that came down to Agnes from her mother included a great deal about Lord Alington:

> The footman who let him in used to tell us that he was always slightly red in the face and flustered, impatient and in a heightened state. We knew he wasn't coming to the house just for a social visit because the rules of etiquette said that married men did not meet married women alone, especially with the curtains drawn in the middle of the afternoon. If there was no sex the Alingtons, man and wife, would have visited Alice together and Alice would have made sure George was there. After all, their whole lives were about socialising so there was no reason for George not to be there; no reason for Lady Alington not to be there unless Mrs Keppel and Lord Alington were lovers, which of course they were.
>
> When Alington arrived the servants knew the couple were not to be disturbed. The butler used to say he could never work out from

the noises whether they were enjoying themselves or inflicting pain on each other!

The affair with Alington was to continue for several years but it ran in tandem with Alice's affair with Lord Stavordale, later the Earl of Ilchester.

Agnes Cook again:

> My mother always said that half the battle for the servants, especially the footmen, was not to laugh at the farcical manoeuvres necessary to keep Alice's various men from bumping into each other. They always thought Alice didn't really like Stavordale that much really but he was very useful as he knew everyone, but especially Bertie, as the Prince of Wales was always known to his friends. I think she liked Alington more and he certainly fell for Alice completely – he used to take her for carriage rides all over London.

Alice loved to be seen in Alington's grand coach. During the intense early period of their relationship he drove her wherever she chose. The trips took in Hampton Court, Kew Gardens and Richmond and regularly on Sundays they would drive along Rotten Row at Hyde Park Corner where the aristocracy paraded their finery while the less exalted watched from a respectable distance.

Famously on one occasion, Alice apparently asked to be driven to see Alington's vast property holdings in the East End of London. He agreed to show her his slum houses. He owned hundreds of run-down, disease-infested properties but refused to spend money repairing them. Instead he racked up the rents as often as he could, although always via various agents. Alice wrote to him afterwards saying how much she had enjoyed herself and looked forward to seeing Hoxton again when it had been improved. It is far more likely that Alice was simply teasing Alington rather than showing a genuine concern for the poor.

Agnes Cook remembered Alice's attitude to her servants and the poor in general:

> I don't think she thought about anyone but herself and her family – and within her family the one she really cared about was her brother Archie, not George and not really the children. We servants got no more nor less than any other servants. The upper classes tried to keep servants' wages down because we were seen as necessary evil – they couldn't do without us but couldn't understand why they had to pay us anything at all! Mrs Keppel couldn't understand why bed and board was not enough and the idea that we might have had lives away from work was completely beyond her. She wasn't especially nasty to us though – it would be unfair to say that. It was just that apart from her lady's maid, who Alice did talk to, the rest of us didn't exist. We were invisible. We didn't matter and that's why she was often so noisy with her male visitors, including later with Edward VII. She would no more have worried about us listening to her goings-on than she would have worried about the sofa listening!

Alington was a good choice as a lover for someone who needed a route to the Prince of Wales. Indeed, he was a personal friend of

Bertie and would no doubt have boasted of the connection and offered to introduce Alice. Nothing would have pleased Alice more. Apart from Beckett, she had increasingly taken lovers who would have filled out the picture of the Prince's life, his likes and dislikes. She would have known long before she met him that he was an especially enthusiastic bridge player and that he was *very* keen on adultery. Alington was just one step from the ultimate goal: the man who would ensure that Alice (not to mention George and her brother Archie) would be immensely wealthy for the rest of her life.

Alice no doubt enjoyed her affairs in the years leading up to her meeting with the Prince of Wales. Certainly she needed to entrance rich men if they were to give her the money she felt she so badly needed, but there was also the need to satisfy her sexual appetites, and her enjoyment of the game, the intrigue. Agnes recalls family gossip which suggests that Alice had at least two other lovers in addition to Stavordale and Alington, and their prime role was not to provide money:

> You have to recall that Alice made it clear to George that she needed him to be absent far more than on the two or three afternoons during the week when either Stavordale or Alington were due to arrive. She also had regular afternoon sessions with a man we never identified – he was tall, good-looking and spoke with a foreign accent. He always came in unannounced and spent an hour or so with

Mrs Keppel. Below stairs we assumed it was perhaps her doctor but the footman always laughed at that and said that if he was a doctor he had a funny way of examining her ladyship!

It seems that Alice Keppel was thoroughly modern in more ways than one. She took the lead role in the family while George drifted about from club to club, and she also enjoyed sex and was determined to get as much of it as possible. She was, if you like, an early groupie – she felt the pull of the famous and knew that by sleeping with them she could enjoy herself and profit at the same time. And profit she certainly did. Towards the end of the 1890s it was noted that the number of diamonds and other jewels she wore increased dramatically; at one ball she dressed in an eighteenth-century outfit so thick with pearls that it was difficult to see the material underneath.

Alice's talent was to amuse and seduce and she knew that these gifts commanded a high price among the bored and idle aristocracy of late nineteenth-century London.

Chapter 4

Bad Boy
Bertie

THERE HAS BEEN much argument about when precisely Alice Keppel met the Prince of Wales, but she probably met him informally at the Keppel family home, Quidenham Hall, in Norfolk in the mid or early 1890s. For whatever reason, Bertie does not seem to have paid any particular attention to her on this occasion. He would have been surrounded by his entourage and she would have sensed that this was not the right time to make a move. Most likely she had yet to hone her seductive strategy, which seems to have gone into overdrive as the 1890s progressed.

Vita Sackville-West claimed that Alice had first properly met the Prince at Lady Howe's house in 1898. Lady Howe, who knew everyone of importance in aristocratic circles, was the daughter of the Duke of Marlborough. It appears that on this occasion the Prince of Wales was immediately struck by Alice's sparkling conversation, which was directed entirely at him, and her striking good looks. From Bertie's point of view Alice had everything: she had beautiful skin, rich chestnut hair, delicately formed hands ... and a large bosom. She was of a type he could never resist. She was also rather short, which made him feel less awkward as he was only 5ft 7in. tall.

Conseulo Vanderbilt, an American unhappily married to the Duke of Marlborough, was to describe Alice's seductive technique in her autobiography, *The Glitter and the Gold* published in 1953. She wrote:

> Her lips were full and her deep throaty voice suggested sensuousness. She had a particular vocal mannerism. Usually she spoke in powerful tones, but when she had a special piece of gossip to emphasise she would allow her voice to drop to a whisper, incline her head and then increase the volume to a sonorous bellow ... she was funny, bright and her flirtatiousness showed a deeply felt liking for men ... When one spoke to her she gave, or seemed to give, the whole of her attention, looking the speaker full in the face.

There is no doubt that Alice and Bertie would have discussed their family connections – Keppels had served the royals in several minor roles over the centuries – and Alice would have brought her considerable charm to bear. At the peak of her social success she 'could have seduced a corpse', according to Agnes Cook. Never lost for words, she was never a bore and always had something amusing to say about everyone.

Other guests at Lady Howe's dinner noted how quickly Bertie and Alice wandered off to enjoy a private conversation. Many were shocked at the speed with which Bertie had succumbed. For more than an hour they stood together at the top of a staircase speaking quietly and intensely and looking continually into each other's eyes. Everyone else was ignored. They then sat down on the top marble step like students in love.

Bertie's private secretary – or 'pimp' as he was described in the radical newspapers of the time – Sir Francis Knollys was brought into play immediately. He was instructed to draft a letter to Alice from Bertie asking if he might call on her. This was always Bertie's code for the first step in seduction.

Even by Alice's standards it was an astonishing coup. It was said that during their initial conversation they had 'reached an understanding' on how their lives would go forward. The request to visit was a coded way of saying 'I wish to visit you for sex so please make sure your husband is absent'.

Ever keen to help both her husband and her brother, Alice had already told Bertie that George would find it easier to be absent during his visit if Bertie would have a word with the Marlborough

Club. The club, one of the most exclusive in London, had pointedly already refused to admit George on several occasions because he was not considered grand enough – many of the members were Dukes and Earls. The ever-obliging Francis Knollys was told by Bertie to tell the club they *must* admit George and within days he was duly accepted as a member.

George was delighted and would have seen nothing wrong in using his wife to gain this kind of preferment. Being a member of the governing classes at this time, as now, was all about influence and connections. In fact, all the evidence suggests that George admired his wife for using her personality and her body to restore the family fortunes while leaving him time to do as he pleased. A friend of his once said: 'George likes nothing more than to tidy up, to buy the latest mechanical toy, to visit his club, to drive in the park. That's it; that's his life. He does no good but at the same time does little harm'.

Agnes Cook recalled George Keppel as an almost ghostly presence, but like Alice and Bertie he enjoyed his life:

> He was vague about almost everything I think, only grumbling if his clothes were not beautifully pressed or if anything in his room was out of place and he never shared a room with Alice – he would have hated it and I think she would too. Aristocrats in those days didn't share bedrooms because they were embarrassed to be seen washing and shaving and so on in front of their spouses and it would have been impossible anyway as George couldn't get dressed without help. He needed his valet. Alice was the same – it took her hours to get ready, bathing and scenting herself and choosing clothes and all with

the help of her lady's maid. If you'd asked Alice if she could manage without a lady's maid she would have thought you were mad. Who would wind her watches? Who would run her bath?

When servants were called up in the First World War she tried to use her influence to keep her servants back – she wrote several letters and I believe the government took note for she always had servants. In those days it was felt that life should not be made difficult for the upper classes even if there was a war on. After all they were seen as unable to manage otherwise. And in this sense George and Alice were helpless – couldn't do a thing for themselves. I don't think Alice Keppel made a cup of tea in her life!

Lord Stavordale and Alice's other lovers may have been a wonderful source of money, but for Alice, Bertie was the ultimate prize. He was also a challenge. He was fifty-eight when they reached their understanding on that staircase in 1898. Alice was twenty-nine. He had spent decades smoking a dozen or more large cigars each day along with as many as twenty cigarettes; at sixteen stone he was massively overweight and appeared to be as wide as he was tall – not difficult to imagine given that he was so short; his beard was invariably stained by nicotine and his past was littered with prostitutes and affairs with other men's wives. To anyone not obsessed by money, power and position he would have seemed an intensely unattractive person; he was a man with only his position to recommend him, but what a position!

All his life he had tried to escape anything that reminded him of his disastrously cruel and intensely boring childhood. As a result, he wanted to be entertained almost continually – he would fly into rages if the entertainment was not good enough or if people failed to act on his wishes; he would snap at his advisers and friends; he would occasionally humiliate them. He liked to pretend that among friends there was no need to stand on ceremony with him but it was not true. He seemed to invite over-familiarity but he never forgave it. Despite his unprepossessing appearance he knew he could do as he liked simply because of his rank. As a man he had nothing to recommend him, but good qualities were simply unnecessary if you were a King-in-waiting.

As well as providing sex and good company Alice Keppel undoubtedly mothered Bertie throughout their relationship, and to find out why he so badly needed mothering we need to look at the long dark history of his parents' lives, his own childhood and his arranged marriage to a woman he would never have chosen himself. If we are to understand Alice Keppel we need to understand the man to whom she devoted the most important years of her life.

Chapter 5

Ugly and Frog-like

WHEN ALBERT EDWARD, eldest son and second child of Queen Victoria, was born on 9 November 1841 the regency was still a recent memory. Queen Victoria's forebears had been rakes and madmen who'd fathered numerous illegitimate children and been pilloried for their gluttony and stupidity in the cartoons of Gillray and Rowlandson and in the newspapers of the time. Princess Victoria was very different. She was not an intellectual but she was a very serious character and throughout her life she was drawn to serious men. She seems to have had a pathological hatred of fun, believing it led to immorality and a weakening of the monarchy. She also believed that the desire for fun and pleasure lay at the heart of the immoral lives of her ancestors, especially the Prince Regent and his circle.

When she married the obscure Prince Albert of Saxe-Coburg and Gotha on 10 February 1840 she found herself attached to a man who was even more serious than she was herself. He believed in work, wrote music that is still occasionally performed today and was an enthusiastic patron of the arts. He was also cold, hard and fiercely puritanical in his dislike of frivolity and excess. He ate little and kept regular hours. His ancestors, like his wife's, had included the most appalling rakes, and Albert's over-serious attitude to life was certainly a reaction to the excesses of his forebears.

Albert's mother and father had both taken a series of lovers and it was his mother's serial adultery that led eventually to her being banished from court while he was still a small child. She was forbidden to see Albert and died aged thirty without setting eyes on him again. This no doubt had an appalling effect on the young Prince and it ensured that, as a man, he insisted on the most rigid standards of conventional conduct. Extramarital relationships had ruined his parents' lives and he was determined that nothing similar would happen to him.

Victoria and Albert wanted their children to be serious and hardworking but they took seriousness too far – and the result for their first-born son was a childhood ruined by an ungenerous, cruel, stupid regime of endless work and no play at all. The irony is that Victoria and Albert's treatment of Bertie produced the very thing they sought to avoid. Instead of the serious scholarly son they had hoped for they ended up with a gluttonous hedonist with no moral compass of any kind. Bertie was to become just as decadent as any of Victoria and Albert's worst ancestors.

Whether Bertie would have been a difficult child anyway is a moot point, but it is certainly true that the daily regime of all work and no play to which he was subjected by a series of largely unsympathetic tutors would probably have turned even the most studious, obedient child into an angry rebel.

<hr />

Bertie came from what today we would call a severely dysfunctional family. Some of course would argue that being a member of the royal family, either now or in previous centuries, is by definition to be part of a dysfunctional family. We only have to look at some of the press interviews given by the late Diana, Princess of Wales, to realise that the royal family resembles the sort of troubled families stereotypically found on the roughest council estates. Diana felt that her husband's infidelity with Camilla Parker Bowles and the royal family's attitude to it was unacceptable, but of course within the royal family infidelity, and the lies and hypocrisy that go with it, has always been de rigueur.

Over the centuries, royal children have always been part of a bizarre world, so outside the norm that its members are often not even aware of how odd they are. This may explain why members of the royal family, despite their privileged upbringings, have developed eccentricities including (in more recent times) talking to plants or referring to 'slitty eyes' while on trips to China.

But among a myriad of dysfunctional royal upbringings, that suffered by Queen Victoria's son Albert Edward must rank as one of the worst. A child treated today as Bertie was treated would be taken into the care of social services; indeed, it was so wicked that it can only be understood if we constantly remind ourselves of Victoria and Albert's own dysfunctional childhoods.

We have no need to go as far back as Charles I or Henry VIII to discover the source of the trouble. Queen Victoria's uncles had the most direct bearing on her attitude to her son. She was brought up to despise and fear her 'wicked uncles', the seven sons of George III. Almost to a man they led lives of unparalleled greed and self-indulgence. Between them they fathered more than twenty illegitimate children yet had no legitimate male heirs.

There is a still a widely held view that has never been entirely disproved that Victoria was herself illegitimate. This stems from the fact that Victoria carried the gene for haemophilia. This gene was not present in either the Saxe-Coburgs or the Hanoverians (her direct ancestors) and it is highly possible that Victoria's mother, the Duchess of Kent, was so desperate for the heir her ageing husband had failed to provide (the Duke of Kent was in his fifties when Victoria was born) that she slept with a much younger member of the royal circle who was sworn to secrecy. Whoever this was is believed to have introduced the rogue gene.

Victoria's strong puritanical streak was a reaction to all this; it was a reaction against the Regency habit of royals fathering children wherever and whenever they could, yet failing to father children with their legitimate wives. Victoria no doubt saw it as a sort of divine punishment. She must have known that her mother had slept with other men – it was widely rumoured and intimately linked to the simple fact that, then as now, the idea of sexual fidelity had never been an important part of life in the British royal family.

Victoria's treatment of Bertie was also a reflection of her own narrow and harsh early years. She was kept a virtual prisoner by her mother, who believed that no scandal should attach to her daughter because there was a very good chance that she would become Queen. George III died in 1820, a few months after Victoria's own father the Duke of Kent had died, and George IV came to the throne. Victoria was now third in line but neither George IV nor any of his ageing brothers was likely to produce an heir.

For seventeen years Victoria stayed in an apartment in Kensington Palace. She slept next to her mother every night and was allowed absolutely no friends her own age. Her governess was specifically chosen because she was German and had no contacts or friends in England. This level of control was precisely what Victoria tried to duplicate in her treatment of her own child many years later. The Duchess of Kent's motivation for treating her daughter in this way has been debated at length. Certainly she felt her daughter should be kept away from bad influences but there was also a more sinister motive. The Duchess wanted a compliant daughter so that if Victoria became Queen while still a minor her mother would be regent.

But William IV (the third son of George III), who became King in 1830 after the death of his brother George IV, seemed curiously unresponsive to the idea of the Duchess becoming regent and she began to suspect that the plan was to cut her out and make Victoria the direct heir. To prevent this, the Duchess kept her daughter as far from court as possible, but it was a regime that made the young Princess difficult and resentful. How ironic then that Victoria should have learned nothing from these early experiences – however much she hated the harshness of her own upbringing she was happy to inflict something remarkably similar on her own son.

Victoria finally escaped from her mother's clutches when William IV died just a few months after Victoria reached the age of eighteen. Her mother's rage at this was unbounded. Victoria immediately wielded her newly found power and left Kensington for Buckingham Palace.

As Queen, Victoria quickly came under pressure to marry and produce a (hopefully) male heir. With her narrow, cloistered upbringing and hatred of anything that reminded her of her mother's loose morals, Victoria was perhaps always bound to pick a controlling, overly serious character.

The British royal family at this time was essentially still German. Her mother had insisted Victoria learn German – she was fluent by the age of ten – and she was taught to consider Germany her spiritual home. Throughout her life she referred to 'dear Germany' and disliked the English aristocracy except insofar as they were good at fulfilling various roles as flunkies. The tradition of looking always to Germany dated back to the first Hanoverian kings, and by the time of George III all male and female members of the royal family were expected to marry their German cousins and to avoid at all costs marrying into the English aristocracy. They turned to minor German royal princedoms – of which there were dozens – and married their relatives, a fact which contributed to pronounced Hanoverian chins (or lack of chins) and a tendency to madness. Victoria herself was convinced that all English monarchs, including her son, should be as German as possible. The German link was only broken after the disaster of the First World War when the royal family became embarrassed by their German connections and were forced to adopt the name Windsor.

So it was no surprise when Victoria met Albert that she fell for him. She had known him long before she became Queen, and members of his family and hers felt the match would be a good one. She proposed in 1839 – as monarch this was her prerogative. She described Albert as 'beautiful' but what really appealed was his deep seriousness that would have become evident after their first meeting. Albert had none of Queen Victoria's ancestors' gluttony; none of their unbridled lust. But Albert's seriousness came at a price; he took himself so seriously that until his death he tried to control Victoria because, though she was Queen, he was a man, and he hated the fact that he had position but no power. Though Victoria looked up to him, she in turn hated the fact that he acted as if he were the monarch, not her. She constantly reminded him that she would not share power, though she did agree to push through the Regency Act of 1840, which stated that in the event of her death Albert would rule as regent in her place until her eldest child reached the age of eighteen. This meant Bertie was no longer next in line to the throne – or at least not until he had come of age.

Victoria and Albert decided early on that with Bertie, if they spared
the rod they would spoil the child; whenever Bertie failed to respond
to his brutal, loveless upbringing she believed it was his fault and
she made it clear she disliked, perhaps even hated him.

Madness is a frequent outcome when family members continually marry each other down the generations. And dysfunctional
attitudes tend to be passed down the generations too – witness
the blighted childhood of the present Prince of Wales, who was
sent to Gordonstoun School in Scotland by his father, the Duke of
Edinburgh, to toughen him up. Charles is on record as saying he
hated the school. Instead of producing the tough sporty adult one
might have expected, Charles became a man who loves conserva-
tion, flowers, wildlife and architecture.

But at least Charles appears to have been welcomed into the world
by his mother. For Bertie things were very different. Probably suffering from what we would now call post-natal depression, Victoria
seems to have disliked him from the outset. But then she appears to
have hated all her children when they were very young. She said she
found babies disgusting and hated their 'frog-like' action.

According to his mother, Bertie as a toddler was 'boring' and she
confided to her diary that he would never be intelligent and noble
enough to justify being called Albert.

At the same time, Victoria was beginning to realise that her husband might prove as much of a trial as her son. Albert saw Victoria
as a child-producing machine and thought it was an absurd quirk
of fate that allowed a mere woman to rule the British Empire when,
as a man, he would have been far better at it. Soon after Bertie was

born he began to try to ensure – just as the Queen's mother had done – that Victoria was kept away from people of whom Albert disapproved. Victoria had exchanged a controlling parent for a controlling husband. Albert saw her as a weak foolish woman who had to be steered through life by a strong serious man, but Victoria resisted many, if not all of his demands throughout their married life. She gave way where it made little difference to her effective role as monarch, making Albert, at his insistence, Prince Consort in 1857.

Albert's interfering, bossy ways made him unpopular with the British public, yet much as she fought with her husband, Victoria continually wrote about how marvellous he was. He would fly into a rage if thwarted or spend days sulking if he could not have his way. Though she was no pushover, Queen Victoria often gave in to his whims, even trying at one point to get Parliament to allow him to use the upgraded title King Consort. Parliament refused.

After their marriage, Albert quickly got rid of Victoria's long-serving governess and oldest friend Baroness Lehzen. He also insisted on changes to the way the royal household was run, eliminating a number of what he saw as anachronistic practices, including the ancient system by which new candles were used every day and the stubs of the old candles were sold by the servants. The servants, who had long seen this as a tiny supplement to their meagre wages, were understandably furious. Albert also introduced his friend and political adviser Baron Stockmar, a German physician with an austere view of life. Together they planned to keep Victoria in her place and under their control, and in time they adopted the same approach with Bertie.

Victoria and Albert blighted Bertie's childhood but they also blighted each other's lives. They simply could not get on – for weeks at a time they would communicate only by letter, even when staying in the same house, and their rows and tantrums were so bad that various members of the court began to believe that Victoria at least might go mad, like George III. When Bertie was warned of the risk he toned down his attacks on her but the truce was only ever temporary.

The only life Victoria had ever known was one where she fought against control. It was her duty to marry but she disliked her husband trying to adopt the traditional male role in the relationship. She also hated babies yet allowed herself to be almost continually pregnant. Why? Well, despite arguing almost continually with Albert, he provided one thing with which she could not do without: sex. She described this part of marriage as 'unbounded happiness … a foretaste of heaven'.

Albert meanwhile had occasional periods when he felt he was getting his way and that there was less need to shout at his Queen. But after each lull the storm soon began again. Even when they were getting on well he could not help his patronising tone that infuriated her – saying on one occasion that he was 'extremely pleased' with the way she was behaving.

The prospects for the young Prince Albert were not good. Both parents made it plain from Bertie's earliest years that they much preferred their first-born child, Victoria, known as Vicky. When she fell ill soon after Bertie was born they were hysterical with grief. They rushed to be with her in a way which is unimaginable with Bertie.

Bertie's earliest experience of a more sympathetic female presence was Laddle, or Lady Lyttelton, the royal governess. Laddle seems to have been hugely indulgent, giving Bertie a brief and no doubt delightful glimpse of what a woman's company might be like. She was indulgent in a way that mirrors precisely Alice Keppel's manner with him. Being ignored by his parents or told that they did not like him as much as they liked their first child made Bertie angry and resentful. Laddle tried to counter this and to make the best of Bertie's slow progress in the schoolroom, but even she struggled with his tantrums.

Curiously he never learned to hate his elder sister Vicky, though he might have been forgiven for seeing her as the author of all his woes. By the time his next sister Alice arrived on the scene in April 1843, he was beginning to learn how to manipulate those around him. Alice grew up with the fixed idea that she must do everything to please her brother and this established a pattern that lasted into adulthood. It was a pattern that was to be repeated with all his mistresses, but especially Alice Keppel.

Bertie's parents always emphasised that Bertie had failed: he had failed to be academically brilliant; he had failed to be musical or interested in the arts; he would never be good enough. Victoria wrote: 'Bertie (I grieve to say) shows more and more how totally, totally unfit he is for ever becoming King.' He had even failed to be good-looking. Victoria said: 'Handsome I cannot think him, with that painfully small and narrow head, those immense features and total want of chin.'

It never perhaps occurred to her that Bertie's physical limitations might be the result of the royal family constantly marrying its own relations. Victoria and Albert were first cousins, which was bound to lead to 'immense features and total want of chin'.

Bertie's answer to endless criticism was to reject everything his parents valued and, having rejected seriousness, he focused his life on pleasure and frivolity. If the world of seriousness, the world of music, the arts and sciences were the worlds valued by his father, his mother and his sister Vicky, then he was having none of it.

Albert thought that German rigour and discipline would make up for Bertie's lack of interest in serious matters. When seriousness and isolation failed to work, he increased the pressure and tried to isolate the already lonely Bertie still further and to make him work longer hours. The harder he pushed the more Bertie resisted.

Albert's friend Baron Stockmar's theories were an overwhelming influence on Bertie's education. They proved disastrous. Stockmar forced the boy to work from eight in the morning until six at night. The Queen's obsession with all things German ensured that German was the first language of the nursery – and to avoid later embarrassment, a speech coach had to be employed when Bertie was a teenager to try to eliminate his German accent in case it was noticed outside the royal circle.

When Bertie was seven, Albert employed a tutor from Eton who had never taught children. Inevitably Henry Birch simply became the next in a line of failed tutors. Indeed, Bertie became ever more wilful, rude and disruptive under Birch's unsympathetic regime, throwing things at him, hiding under tables and refusing to come out. Today Bertie might well have been diagnosed as suffering from Attention Deficit Hyperactivity Disorder (ADHD) but he may also have genuinely struggled to learn (inbreeding had not so far produced many great royal thinkers) and besides, he would have known that his place in society was assured whatever he learned or did not learn, simply because of the accident of his birth.

Any kind of motivation must be difficult when you grow up knowing your life is already mapped out in front of you. Certainly in more recent times the lives of the children of Queen Elizabeth have suggested this might well be the case. Prince Charles was not hugely motivated at school and was lucky that royal influence was brought to bear to get him into Cambridge with A level grades that would have ensured instant rejection for lesser mortals. His great-great-grandfather Bertie had the same advantages – and disadvantages.

Bertie's realisation that he would one day be King and that attempts to make him studious would make no difference to this outcome, resulted in a child who hated study and work; he was a rebel who tried his best to avoid doing anything he didn't want to do. Eventually Albert became so frustrated that he had Bertie whipped.

The beatings made no difference and, as Bertie dug his heels in, so his father tried ever more extreme measures. Bertie was allowed no friends his own age; indeed, no friends at all. The wonder is that he did not go mad or try to murder his tutor.

Albert became so desperate he called in a phrenologist to test the bumps on Bertie's head to look for signs of that old Hanoverian malady – madness. The phrenologist told Albert his son's brain was not properly formed. Albert confided to his diary that Bertie must be treated as a mental patient.

※——※※——※

Bertie's tutor Henry Birch was a dogmatic and self-serving man who seems to have spent most of his time badgering Albert for favours and preferment. But he wasn't entirely stupid. When he saw that beatings and severity failed to work, he tried a gentler approach and found that Bertie at last responded and began to make progress.

In the mad world inhabited by the royals this new approach made Albert furious. Being kind to Bertie was an example of weak, self-indulgent behaviour. Birch was immediately sacked and a new tutor – the gruesome Frederick Gibbs – was drafted in from Cambridge.

Within weeks of Birch's departure Bertie's behaviour had deteriorated to such an extent that Gibbs began to fear for his safety. Bertie threw everything he could get his hands on at the new tutor, he shouted insults at him and terrified visitors by firing blank cartridges at them from his shotgun. Albert suggested more beatings. Various advisers, including Lord Clarendon and Bertie's German teacher, tried to intervene and suggested that Bertie should be treated with kindness and allowed to mix with boys his own age. Albert and Victoria disagreed and the cruelty continued. Eventually it seems that Victoria and Albert were convinced that the Hanoverian madness was so much a part of Bertie that nothing could be done – except further beatings.

By the time he was in his mid-teens Bertie had learned to be out-wardly conformist with his tutors while subverting their efforts in less obvious ways than he had adopted as a child. He learned to be devious and to treat rules and regulations simply as obstacles to negotiate so that he could have fun. He learned to appear to do as he was told while inwardly planning to do as he wished. He had grown used to the endless stream of letters from his mother to his sister Vicky complaining about his inadequacies; he had learned to tolerate his parents, but he must have been surprised, nonetheless, when, at the age of fifteen, he heard that his father had finally agreed that the harsh regime he had endured for so long was to be eased. He would at least be allowed occasionally to travel.

In 1857, when he was sixteen, Bertie was packed off to Germany for a few months to appease his mother, who insisted that a British monarch should have as much as possible in common with a Ger-man Prince. A hint of scandal drifted back to England when it was discovered that Bertie had kissed a girl. Worse was to come when, early in 1859 during a visit to Italy, Bertie was discovered to have written a love letter to Lady Churchill, a beautiful lady-in-waiting twenty years his senior.

It was an early sign of the pattern of things to come.

Tutors gave way at last to what Queen Victoria and Albert called Bertie's 'governor'. This was Colonel Robert Bruce and in the autumn of 1859 Bertie was forced to accompany Bruce to Oxford. Bertie had no formal qualifications but was allowed to study as an undergraduate at Christ Church. When he attended lectures (always in the company of Bruce) the other students were forced to stand, yet at no time of day or night was he allowed out of the Colonel's sight. He still had no friends and Victoria insisted he should not be allowed to mix with other undergraduates at all lest they lead him into any temptations. But at least one undergraduate slipped through the net; Bertie made friends with Sir Frederick Johnstone, who drank, smoked, gambled and womanised. At last Bertie had a soul mate.

It was probably Bertie's relationship with his sister Alice that kept him sane during his long and painful childhood. Alice always thought well of him; always indulged him and made it clear that whatever others thought of him she admired and loved him. She also conspired with him to some extent against the Queen. Alice was the pattern of all those women Bertie was later to be drawn to. Colonel Bruce, Gibbs and Henry Birch were the pattern of serious worthy men Bertie spent his later life avoiding.

But by the time he reached Oxford, Bertie was increasingly aware of his power as heir to the throne. It was not just the deference of those with whom he came into contact – fellow students, lecturers and others – it was the dazzled and excited looks of passers-by, especially women. Bertie was famous simply because of who he was and despite his minute stature. He was famous for being famous and, rather like a modern rock star, he was determined by the age of sixteen to use his fame to sleep with as many women as possible.

In their desperate attempts to make Bertie more serious, Victoria and Albert decided that, having studied at Oxford, he should have another dose of academia at Cambridge. But first in the summer of 1860, when Bertie was eighteen, he was sent on a tour of Canada and the United States where he was lionised and where local newspapers reported his flirtations with a number of young women.

It is impossible now to know if these flirtations involved sexual intercourse, but given how keen the Americans were to please him and how far he was from the eyes of his parents, it is highly likely. A report in the *New York Herald* suggested that Bertie had more than flirted with the ladies, but there was no proof. The anonymous writer merely commented that 'His Royal Highness had yielded to twinges in his midriff!'

Back from America Bertie was filled with a zest for life that seemed entirely new in him. His whirlwind tour of America and his success there also gave him a lifelong taste for travel – travel and sex and the sex that travel allowed were to fill his adult years.

That autumn Bertie was escorted to Cambridge for another year's hated study. Colonel Bruce was so determined to follow Victoria's commands to the letter – especially after rumours of Bertie's behaviour in America had reached her – that he rented a house well outside Cambridge where he and the Prince could live in seclusion, thereby avoiding any risk that Bertie should meet or spend any time with fellow students.

But the chains that held Bertie were weakening, and even if the young Prince could not be described as academically bright he was certainly cunning. As time passed his cunning increased. He had learned that outward conformity would keep Colonel Bruce happy, even if inwardly Bertie despised the older man and made every effort to escape him.

Cambridge was to supply Bertie with his first extended experience of sex and it had such a profound effect on him that from then on he made it his life's work to seek it out wherever and whenever he could. It was a pleasure that was to become vital to Bertie's every waking moment. He always enjoyed food, wine and smoking it is true, but sex was his drug of choice.

A Rake's Progress

*I*N LATER LIFE Bertie often had several mistresses on the go at any one time both during his long wait to become King and during much of his reign. He never lost his taste for prostitutes either and, on his numerous trips abroad, he was frequently seen emerging from brothels, especially in Paris and Hamburg where such establishments were perfectly legal.

Bertie's sexual appetites were extraordinary by any standards. It has been said, with how much truth it is difficult to say, that much of Bertie's sex life involved a few fumblings followed by a cup of tea. This may have been true when he was so fat that he needed to use a special harness to have any chance of experiencing penetrative sex, but it seems highly unlikely to be true of his early years, given the number of women he was linked to, his liking for brothels and his numerous illegitimate children.

But Bertie's desperation for sex may also be linked to what might best be termed a Freudian issue with his anatomy. Ralph Martin in *The Women He Loved* quotes a friend of Bertie's saying: 'To put it bluntly he had the smallest pecker I've ever seen.'

There is no doubt that Bertie's principal aim in life was to enjoy women, and that aim was first properly formulated at Cambridge. Despite being locked away from temptation it seems he managed to escape his jailer to meet the gambling, smoking and hunting set, which included Nathaniel Rothschild and Charles Lord Carrington. Carrington, who was to become a lifelong friend, suggested that Bertie escape at night from his governor through a window of the isolated house at Madingley. He would then be taken by Carrington and the others to various parties and drinking houses in Cambridge before returning at dawn. At one of these parties Carrington engaged the services of a young woman and part-time actress called Nellie Clifden. Nellie's role was to have sex with Bertie and probably any of the other young men who could pay.

The year 1861 was a good one for Bertie. It was the year in which life must have seemed to begin to open up for him. It was the year of his first sexual experience. He had already been allowed to smoke and he took to it with a passion that was never to leave him. He had toured North America, studied – if that is the right word – at Oxford and Cambridge, and was then allowed to visit the military camp at the Curragh in Ireland.

Bertie must have thought soldiering was a splendid life because his quarters turned out to be a suite of rooms. The soldiers slept in tents. And though he was guarded night and day by the sinister Colonel Bruce, he had clearly made friends with the sort of people he was always to be drawn to for the rest of his life – he loved mischievous, fun-loving officers who liked to kick over the traces; men and women who knew the rules but also knew how to break them.

Despite the destruction of Bertie's papers, odd bits of his correspondence do turn up now and again. There are a few appointment books, and among the most interesting references to be found in these so far are a few coded notes in an engagement diary. The person referred to is NC, clearly Nellie Clifden. Bertie was guarded enough as a twenty-year-old to use only her initials, but he was to be far more guarded later on after a series of bruising encounters with irate husbands.

NC is listed against three dates in 1861 when Bertie was at the military camp in Ireland: 6 September, 9 September and 10 September. It seems most likely that on these three nights the Prince arranged with a fellow officer that he should climb through a window in the dead of night and make his way to another officer's hut. There the delightful Nellie Clifden, specially brought over from

England for the purpose, was waiting with instructions (and a generous payment) to make sure the Prince had some fun.

Kept away from pleasures of all kinds for so long and clearly highly sexed, Bertie knew, after sleeping with Nellie, that he had found his reason for living. If it is true that all men desire power and sex, Bertie, denied any real power until he was nearly sixty, focused all his attention as an adult on the sexual part of the equation. After Nellie, he devoted his life to the pursuit of women. It might be argued that Bertie's long list of liaisons was to be an attempt to recover the excitement of those first couplings with Nellie Clifden. The society women he endlessly seduced in later life appealed both as surrogate mothers and as sexual partners, but Nellie was a professional and Bertie's pleasure was untainted by any claims, other than financial ones. Other mistresses caused trouble because they wanted more than money, but Alice Keppel, like Nellie Clifden, made no such demands.

Even while he was having sex with Nellie, Bertie was aware that if his parents discovered what he was up to he would be in utter disgrace. He would also have known that his father and mother and his sister Vicky were conspiring to ensure he was married off as soon as possible. As ever, the British-German royal family – a family that hated the idea of losing its direct links with Germany – was determined to avoid finding a match for Bertie among the English aristocracy.

A German Princess would therefore have to be found, but the matchmakers quickly discovered that this would not be easy. The few

German Princesses Vicky was able to track down were either mad or bad or both. Anna of Hesse, who was about the right age, was considered, but she had appalling teeth and a moustache and spoke with a voice deeper than that of a man. Elisabeth of Wied was also considered but she was a tomboy – loud, boastful and manically talkative.

Vicky knew her parents would want someone for Bertie who was quiet and obedient and the reason for this had as much to do with Victoria and Albert wanting to control their daughter-in-law as it had with any concern for their son's future happinesss. Victoria and Albert's desire to control every aspect of their son's life, even when he was a young adult made any prospect of a love match impossible.

It was a pattern of control that a more recent generation of royals was to repeat disastrously in the marriage of Prince Charles in 1981 to Lady Diana Spencer. In this relationship the royal family and its advisers agreed to allow Charles to marry Diana on the basis that she was seen as quiet and likely to be uncomplaining should Charles insist on the royal prerogative to have affairs. In Bertie's case the royal bride turned out to be just as complaisant as everyone had hoped; in the case of Diana, as we know, the misjudgement was so wide of the mark that it almost destroyed the monarchy.

When Victoria and Albert chose Princess Alexandra of Denmark, the selection was entirely due to Alexandra's personal qualities of meekness and mildness. From a political point of view, the choice was controversial because the Danish royal family had long ago fallen out with the Prussians over rival claims to the territory familiar to every schoolboy historian: Schleswig-Holstein.

But in the absence of any suitable German Princess, Victoria and Albert were determined Bertie should marry Alexandra. An initial meeting was arranged casually during a visit to Germany in September 1861, ostensibly organised so that Bertie could study military manoeuvres. The couple met at Speyer Cathedral on the Rhine. Bertie complained she was less attractive than the rather flattering portrait he had already seen, but was told he was being absurd.

Bertie's lack of real enthusiasm enraged his father, who shouted at his son at Windsor later that year, insisting it would be disgraceful not to propose to Alexandra when she came to Windsor. Meanwhile the family's German relatives were furious when they discovered what was planned. They were appalled that a German Princess, whatever the state of her teeth, was to be overlooked. They wrote to Albert insisting that Alexandra's mother was a whore and her father a lunatic. Albert, who was half in love with Alexandra himself by now, told his relatives it was none of their business.

Throughout the dull business of his family finding a bride for him, Bertie did as he had always done in earlier days when bored to distraction in the classroom – he outwardly conformed while inwardly making his own plans, plans that had nothing to do with these dynastic arrangements.

Bertie's childhood was by all accounts so unhappy that it is arguable his later eating, drinking and womanising were simply attempts to blot out the past. The raw horror of those early days can be judged by the fact that, when his mother finally died, Bertie immediately threw out her most treasured possessions, turned Osborne House into a naval college and had all Victoria's and Albert's papers put away in the archives; their pictures and photographs consigned to storage. He wanted nothing at Windsor or Buckingham Palace to remind him of the past.

✳━✳✳━✳

Bertie was nearly twenty. It was now almost impossible to control him night and day because he fully understood his position as Prince of Wales and the spell this enabled him to cast on others; so long as his parents were not around he knew he could get his way.

He began by asking his friends to organise a special celebration for him on his twentieth birthday, 9 November 1861. The venue was to be Windsor Castle and the party was, as it were, Bertie's reward to himself for enduring his trip to Germany to meet Alexandra. On his return from that first meeting and following several uncomfortable discussions with his father in which the marriage was presented to him as an absolute necessity, Bertie desperately wanted to have fun. So he made sure his friends, principally Natty Rothschild and Carrington, brought Nellie Clifden to London and then on to Windsor where he was able to have sex with her again. Bertie's rakish friends knew that a few hours with Nellie Clifden was the only present the Prince would really want.

When the young men arrived with Nellie, the guards and other officials at Windsor were either bribed or too overawed to question the aristocratic group. Bertie seems to have enjoyed the fact that Nellie was having sex with him *and* with his friends. It made the encounters entirely guilt-free. She made no demands on him, although she spent months joking to anyone who would listen that *she* was now the Princess of Wales.

But the storm clouds were gathering. Somehow rumours began to spread that Nellie had been at Dublin and at Windsor Castle for Bertie's birthday and the gossip became increasingly lurid – it was said that Nellie had cavorted naked in front of Bertie and his friends; that she had disappeared for twenty minutes at a time with one officer then another, then Bertie. It was rumoured that Bertie specifically asked to enjoy Nellie's favours after the others. The main source of the gossip when it finally reached Victoria and Albert appears to have been Lord Torrington, who no doubt enjoyed being the bearer of exciting if devastating news.

Victoria and Albert's reaction, even by the standards of the time, seems overblown. Victoria said she would never get over it; she claimed she was even more upset because Albert was upset. It was as if the long shadow of their sexually rapacious ancestors had finally caught up with them despite all their efforts to crush any sign of it in their first-born son. Albert insisted sex was a 'sacred mystery', that it should be shrouded in 'holy awe'. One can only imagine Bertie inwardly hooting at this.

The truth is that though Albert enjoyed sex, he could not bear to think of it outside marriage and, worse, with someone of another class. Nellie was, in his view, the lowest of the low; a 'defilement' – just the sort of woman his own father would have spent his life running after.

Having heard the rumours, Albert immediately wrote to Bertie, who was back at Cambridge. His letter was a crude attempt at moral blackmail. It is filled with self-pity; filled with the story of how Albert, the perfect father, has been wronged by the ungrateful son. In a wonderfully melodramatic passage, Albert says he cannot believe that Bertie would willingly thrust himself into 'the hands of one of the most abject of the human species'. Without mentioning Nellie by name, he points out that she is just the sort of woman who might easily end up blackmailing Bertie. And in this sense at least, Albert was right, because soon after the scandalous birthday party at Windsor, a local man contacted the palace to claim his wife had been seduced by Bertie. Panic-stricken, the palace agreed to pay the man, a Mr Green, and his wife £60 a year for life, but only on condition they went to live in New Zealand.

This kind of problem was to be a regular nightmare for the palace throughout Bertie's adulthood and reign. He was like Mr Toad, always getting into scrapes and then having to be rescued by the occasional illegal manoeuvrings of palace officials, who always took the view that Bertie was never the villain, he was simply being manipulated; he was the victim and had been trapped by unscrupulous low-class people. Bertie was never to blame. In his parents' eyes, on the other hand, Bertie was *always* to blame.

Albert had been brought up entirely by men after his mother was banished from the court. He had an almost monastic view of sex, and though he clearly enjoyed it, there is no record of him ever having sex with anyone other than Victoria. He must have known, however, that most young male aristocrats in Victorian times resorted regularly to prostitutes. So long as they did it fairly discreetly it was perfectly socially acceptable.

Sex with children for money was especially popular among the aristocracy. In his book *Winter Notes on Summer Impressions* Dostoevsky recalls a visit to London at the end of the nineteenth century. He describes the throng of poverty-stricken mothers selling little girls for sex in London's Haymarket. Most of the buyers were top-hatted aristocrats. Officialdom denied a problem existed until the *Pall Mall Gazette* editor W. T. Stead bought a thirteen-year-old girl in the Haymarket for £5 to prove it really was happening. He was prosecuted for drawing the authorities' attention to something they preferred to pretend did not exist.

Officially, of course, prostitution of any kind was always frowned upon. The beautiful colonnade that once ran along John Nash's Regent Street was demolished at about this time because it was said to provide shelter for vast numbers of prostitutes of all ages waiting for their wealthy clients to finish eating in the Café Royal and elsewhere. Hyde Park and Green Park were famous for their older prostitutes. Worn out and diseased by early middle age, these women would offer more sophisticated pleasures including oral sex. In the dark it didn't matter what they looked like and the parks had the great advantage of being just a stone's throw from the grand London houses of the English upper classes in Mayfair and the Prince of Wales's home at Marlborough House.

Victorian England was above all hypocritical. So long as a man appeared to be respectable he could do as he pleased. Only Albert, a German, failed to see this. The English upper classes were regular churchgoers but they allowed children to work for sixteen hours a day in mines and factories. They insisted their wives and daughters were too delicate for work, yet their twelve-year-old maids worked eighty and more hours each week. It was a world that started a revolution – the unconventional lifestyles adopted by members of the Bloomsbury Group are a good example of a limited attempt to rebel against this hypocrisy. Bertie, however, did not rebel in quite the same way.

Confronted by Albert he confessed to his philandering and promised to mend his ways. He played the part of the prodigal son; he went through the show of repentance but clearly not meaning a word of it. He allowed his father to believe that somehow he had been led astray by others.

Victoria saw Bertie's failure as a confirmation of all her predictions and she was almost as pleased to find she had been right all along as she was disgusted by his behaviour. No wonder that through her long reign she refused absolutely to allow him any share in her official duties. Practically her sole concession to the fact that he would one day be King was to allow him to tour America and Canada and even then she afterwards felt she had made a mistake in allowing him to go.

Though she argued constantly with her husband, Victoria was obsessed by the idea that he was godlike in his purity and brilliance. Her belief in him was almost pathological and it was Albert's distress at Bertie's affair with Nellie Clifden that inflamed her already low opinion of her eldest son.

When Torrington spilled the beans on the affair, Albert was unwell. He had visited his old home at Coburg in Germany a year earlier. While on that visit he'd had to jump from his carriage when the horses bolted. He was badly shaken and developed stomach pains as a result. He also dreaded his return to England; he hated England for not allowing him to be King and by now he also hated himself for being fat and bald.

At the end of November 1861, having written his pathetic letter, Albert, still unsure that Bertie really had learned his lesson, set off by train for Cambridge. For reasons that are unclear, Albert insisted he and Bertie should go for a walk to discuss the young man's behaviour. It seems odd that Albert should have suggested this as he was already ill and it was a miserably cold, wet day.

They patched up their relationship after a talk that lasted into the early hours of the morning and Albert was soon back in Windsor, but what had been a mild cold suddenly worsened. Victoria blamed Bertie, Bertie blamed the weather. By early December it was clear that Albert was suffering from typhoid, almost certainly caused by the medieval sewage system at Windsor. His soaking a month earlier in Cambridge had merely exacerbated his symptoms. Bertie later contracted typhoid but, unlike his father, he recovered. Albert rapidly deteriorated and died on 14 December. He was just forty-two.

Terrified of Victoria and convinced they would be blamed, Albert's doctors suggested that his fever had been made untreatable by his mental state – a state caused by Bertie's bad behaviour with Nellie Clifden. Victoria seized on this, blamed the whole thing on Bertie and settled down to more than forty years of bitter, reclusive mourning.

The vacuum created by Albert's death could have been filled by Bertie, but Victoria was having none of it; just as she had destroyed Bertie's childhood, so now with Albert dead she was determined to

punish him and to deny him a constitutional role. She said: 'That boy...
I never can or ever shall look at him without a shudder.'

The inevitable result was that Bertie, idle and bored, threw himself into the role he liked best – that of a philandering glutton.

For all her histrionics, the truth is that Victoria probably preferred
Albert dead to Albert alive. She could now play the self-indulgent
role of the tragic Queen and use his death as an excuse for pun-
ishing Bertie and retiring from public view. With Albert gone she
could forget all the annoying details of their life together. His sulks
and rages had driven her to distraction along with his endless complaints that he should have more power. Now that he was dead he
could be turned into a golden idol, the widowed Queen uphold-
ing the notion that, unlike most of her male ancestors and her son,
Albert was virtually a saint.

Bertie, too, was almost certainly pleased on some level that his
father had died. Albert had beaten and whipped him as a child, controlled and scolded him as an adult. Bertie played the role of grieving
son and had even agreed to stop seeing Nellie Clifden, but he had
absolutely no intention of changing the way he planned to live. With
Albert out of the way it would just be easier. Nellie Clifden, and
all the other women with whom he was to become involved, represented pleasure, frivolity and fun; everything Albert hated.

But like Alice Keppel, Bertie had to be married in order to fully
engage with the adult world. He would no doubt have chosen a

voluptuous, sexually forthcoming woman. His mother's choice for him, Princess Alexandra, did not fit the bill. She was very thin, sexually timid, overly serious and concerned only to do her duty.

Outwardly conforming as ever, Bertie reconciled himself to the fact that his mother would have her way in this. If she said he must marry Alexandra he would do it, but he also knew that the marriage would not stop him doing as he pleased; it would be a sham, a dynastic arrangement. He would go through with it but he would get his revenge. He knew that, once married, he could and would continue to sleep with other women whatever the feelings of his wife on the matter.

Bertie would quickly have become aware that, of all possible wives, Alexandra would be least likely to interfere in any effective way with his philandering, so she was as good a choice as any who fitted the role as defined by his mother.

He no longer needed tantrums to try to get his way. He would simply do as he pleased now that his mother had retired almost completely from public life. He would never actually confront Alexandra with his lifestyle. Instead he would move from house party to house party, always drinking, eating, gambling and smoking and always with his own group of friends.

The world in which Nellie and Bertie's rakish friends moved was the world of gambling, promiscuity and partying; precisely the world that his parents hated.

While the marriage plans continued, Victoria was determined to get rid of Bertie, so she sent him on a four-month tour of the Middle East in early 1862. Bertie travelled first to Venice, which he enjoyed, and then on to Egypt where he studiously avoided museums and ancient ruins and seems to have spent his time shooting at birds and animals he spotted from his Nile cruiser, and playing cards.

Meanwhile, whether locked away in the shrine of rooms she had created at Windsor in memory of Albert or in the gloomy corridors of Osborne House on the Isle of Wight, his mother was enjoying making the Danish royal family feel inferior and reminding Princess Alexandra that she was therefore very lucky to have the chance to marry her son.

She felt the Danish royal family was beneath her simply because they were not German. When Alexandra was summoned to the Isle of Wight, the rest of the family was told that only Alexandra would be welcome. Alexandra's father was not even introduced to Victoria; instead he was simply banished to a hotel.

But the tables were turned when Princess Alexandra's mother, Princess Louise, had second thoughts about the marriage after discovering that Bertie had been having sex with Nellie Clifden and other prostitutes.

Disgusted that she had to defend her wayward son, Victoria nonetheless did so, insisting that Bertie was an innocent who had been schemed against by lesser mortals. It was the old lie, but it would do. For Victoria the pressure was now on to get the marriage fixed and over with as soon as possible. Bertie, who was never consulted, seems to have gone along with the whole thing good-humouredly, safe in the knowledge that, as he later put it, Alexandra was really only his 'brood mare' after all. Servicing his brood mare was all about duty; servicing Alice Keppel was to be all about pleasure.

He knew there was no point in direct resistance to his mother. Victoria had seen Alexandra and decided, 'she will suit me'. Meanwhile, playing a part as in all communication with his mother, Bertie was soon claiming that he was 'head over heels' in love with Alexandra or 'Alix' as the Queen was soon addressing the Danish Princess. But Bertie almost overdid it when he wrote to Victoria, 'I did not think it possible to love a person as I do her'. It was all part of a tactic he had learned long ago to never oppose his mother directly. But then if she dominated him, perhaps it was only fair, as he dominated everyone else and especially his friends. He had learned from his mother how to get his way.

On his trip down the Nile, for example, he had made everyone in his entourage read the same novel – a novel about adultery. And like his mother he was to brook no opposition; in his case, opposition to the pursuit of pleasure.

If Bertie had been humiliated as a child he could certainly, as an adult, humiliate others. He could also be very rude to those he felt were not prepared to always let him have his way. Francis Knollys, his private secretary, even had to lie for him. The alternative was that he would be replaced.

On 10 March 1863, Bertie and Alexandra were married. He was twenty-one, she was just eighteen. This was one of the great moments of Bertie's liberation. He may not have wanted to marry but he quickly realised that, far from curtailing his freedom, marriage actually extended it. In the world of late nineteenth-century hypocrisy, Bertie could please his mother by fathering children, and so long as he remained married he could pursue other women to his heart's content.

Marriage gave Bertie the formal status of maturity, but it was a facade; many, including no doubt his mother, believed that if his sexual energies were legitimately focused within marriage, the philandering would stop. As so often with anything to do with Victoria, the law of unforeseen consequences took over and the result was very different from anything of which she would have approved.

※—※—※

Bertie and Alexandra set off for their honeymoon at Osborne House on the Isle of Wight, arranged, as everything else about the marriage had been arranged, by Victoria. At Osborne the grim rooms revealed that everything had been left as it was in Albert's time; their honeymoon took place in what was effectively a mausoleum.

Victoria had told the couple while they were standing in front of Albert's grave on the day before the wedding that her dead husband, Bertie's father, had given them his blessing; it was as if Bertie was being warned that, even in death, Albert would be watching him. And not only Albert. Victoria's need to control had never left her and she insisted that secret reports be filed on the couple by the flunkeys and retainers at Osborne House, Sandringham and Balmoral.

Bertie, so far as she was concerned, could never be trusted. Lists of the couple's dinner guests had to be sent to the Queen for approval; if Alexandra wanted to ride in the park, that too had to be approved by the old Queen. It was as if, bored of her limited political power, the monarch was making up for it by ensuring she had power over her son and his wife, not to mention her other children. And while this was all going on, Victoria wrote repeatedly to her daughters, but especially Vicky, to say that Bertie was idle and utterly unfit to become King. Even in the deepest recesses of Windsor Castle, word soon reached her in the months after her son's marriage that Bertie never read a book, that he gambled, stayed up late, visited the theatre and mixed with prostitutes and what she called the 'fast set', and dedicated himself to eating, drinking and – a relatively new passion – shooting.

✣⟶❈⟶✣

In London the newlyweds lived at Marlborough House, just along The Mall from Buckingham Palace. This beautiful house, built by Sir Christopher Wren, was immediately refurbished at a staggering cost: Parliament voted £60,000 for the work, which destroyed a great deal of the original interior in favour of work by the now largely forgotten architect James Pennethorne.

From the time the couple moved into Marlborough House, Princess Alexandra was treated as if she was there for one reason and one reason only. Everyone, from her doctor to Bertie, from the ladies-in-waiting to the Queen, was kept fully informed about whether she was having a period or not so that Bertie could be forbidden from organising dinners and parties at these times. Indeed, throughout the couple's early marriage, there was an obsession in the royal household with Alexandra's bodily functions – hardly surprising, then, that Bertie was never able to see beyond his judgement that she was simply his brood mare.

In fact, Alexandra fell pregnant fairly quickly after the marriage and on 8 January 1864, a boy was born. The couple were bullied by the old Queen into christening the child Albert Victor. He was to die mired in sexual scandal while still only in his twenties.

Bertie was probably genuinely delighted at the birth of an heir, but he would also have been immensely relieved – he would have known that failure to make Alix pregnant would have been seen as another personal failure on his part. Throughout the Princess's pregnancy and through her next five pregnancies, Bertie was largely absent. He continued to see his old friends Carrington and Natty Rothschild and set the pattern for a mode of life that was to continue until his death. He gambled and visited prostitutes, but the great loves of his life, loves that were to culminate in Alice Keppel, were only just entering his world.

There seems little doubt that, despite the arranged marriage, Bertie became very fond of Alix – she was, after all, largely uncomplaining and to a remarkable extent let him do, throughout his life, exactly as he pleased.

Meanwhile Alix's every move continued to be monitored by Victoria. She appointed three doctors to look after the Princess, but then insisted that she knew best and told the doctors precisely how Alix was to be treated. The medical regime involved treating Alix as if she were an invalid child: she was made to go to bed at precisely the same time each night and forced to take a daily walk, whether she wished to or not. Victoria was like a great octopus whose powerful tentacles were everywhere. She was also remarkably insensitive, complaining bitterly about everything Bertie did and then lamenting the fact that he would not confide in her. Alix, on the other hand, was so mild-mannered that Victoria adored her.

Whenever he went abroad Bertie felt he had escaped the octopus's tentacles, and this was when he was most likely to get into trouble. In 1864 he visited Copenhagen with Alix to see her parents, but refused to travel under a false name as Victoria had instructed. She was furious and forbade Bertie from coming back via Paris, where he no doubt intended to enjoy the pleasures of the city's legendary brothels with which he was already familiar.

Because he was allowed no serious constitutional role, he became obsessed, as Prince Charles today is sometimes said to be obsessed, with trivia. He insisted, for example, that everyone at his weekend parties should dress exactly as he dictated. He was meticulous about his own appearance and even made turn-ups on trousers fashionable – it was a sartorial response to his habit of rolling his trousers up to cross muddy fields during shoots.

The habit of slavishly copying anything the monarch did continued when the increasingly fat Bertie found he could no longer do up the bottom button of his waistcoat. Soon everyone who aspired to great things began leaving their bottom buttons undone – a trend that persists to this day.

Bertie gambled heavily while in Paris and Hamburg – ignoring his mother's instructions to avoid Paris – and delighted in his occasional huge losses. He lost more than £130 in one short evening session at the casino, an amount that would have kept a working-class family for a year or two.

He also devoted his money to lavish rebuilding at Sandringham, simply relying on the ever-willing Knollys to come up with the money. As Prince of Wales he felt he should have as much money as he wanted and was outraged when Knollys told him that Parliament would not necessarily acquiesce in all his spending plans. There were signs, too, that Bertie was beginning to flex his muscles. He had done his marital and dynastic duties and he felt he deserved something in return. He told his mother he wanted to use the regnal name Edward rather than Albert when he eventually became King (she was furious) and that he would christen his second son George whether the Queen agreed or not. She did not – she had wanted the next male child to be called Albert. Indeed, if she could have had her way all Bertie's sons would have been called Albert. Bertie once again refused and the Queen, perhaps for the first time in her life, realised that in some matters she could no longer get her way. But there was still much to be enjoyed in the power she wielded in trivial matters.

Bertie gathered his favourite cronies at Windsor for his twenty-third birthday celebration in 1864. The party had hardly got going when the old Queen ordered everyone to bed at eleven o'clock.

On the surface Bertie put up with this sort of thing but underneath he seethed. Years later towards the end of his mother's life in 1897, he commented ruefully, 'I don't mind praying to the eternal father, but I must be the only man in the country afflicted with an eternal mother.'

A form of escapism was provided by shooting, of which he became very fond. Pheasant shooting at Sandringham and at the houses of his aristocratic friends was as brutal a business in the late nineteenth century as it is today. The relatively recent invention of the breech-loading shotgun meant guns could be loaded quickly and more birds could therefore be shot. The sport, if sport is the right word, turned into slaughter on a colossal scale. And there was huge collateral damage. In order to rear tens of thousands of pheasants successfully for the guns, birds of prey and other predators were ruthlessly extirpated. Five or six thousand pheasants might be killed in a day by a team of just ten guns along with as many as five or six hundred hares, countless rabbits, jays, woodpigeons, woodcocks and almost anything else that moved. And such days might be repeated as many as a dozen times in a season.

Bertie was always told he was a fine shot, but early copies of the *Shooting Times* record that it would have been generous to call him average. As one writer observed: 'With the air black with rising birds it was hard even for the Prince of Wales to miss everything.'

Shoots were organised like military operations with pheasants reared in vast numbers before being released into woodland. On the shoot day, a long line of beaters would drive the birds towards the 'gentlemen guns' spaced out along the bottom of a valley or on the edge of the wood. The guns had little to do but stand and shoot before being carried to the next drive or to an elaborate and lengthy lunch.

For Bertie, shooting was one of the few activities he enjoyed that was largely beyond the reach of his mother and it was one in which he could meet and plan with his fellow rakes and cronies.

All through his life his mother had written furious letters about Bertie's behaviour and this continued throughout the years of his marriage. When Bertie or her other children agreed with her, Victoria praised them extravagantly, but the least disagreement would lead to a furious correspondence, with key words in each letter underlined once, twice or three times.

Bertie was almost always out of favour but, occasionally, if one of Victoria's daughters happened to be insufficiently obedient, then Bertie, for a short time, would become the royal favourite. Bertie presented one side of his personality to his mother and another to the rest of the world. Even while he was sleeping with the wives of his friends and regularly visiting Parisian brothels, he told his mother in their rare interviews that he was endeavouring to devote his life to emulating his late father.

Chapter 7

Stormclouds

WITHIN A FEW years of marriage Princess Alexandra developed a severe arthritic knee. She then gradually lost her hearing. She became a permanent semi-invalid – and deafness was to plague her for the rest of her life. There has always been speculation that Bertie passed syphilis to his wife and certainly some, if not all, of Alix's symptoms seem to fit such a diagnosis: the 'arthritic knee' was actually a massive ulcer on the Princess's lower leg, and ulcers and deafness were key indicators of syphilis.

Whatever the truth of the matter, it would have been remarkable if Bertie had not passed on a venereal disease of some sort to his wife, given his passion for prostitutes. And it seems that Bertie really only spent time with Alix when he came home from his jaunts to sleep with her for short periods. So much is clear from a letter Victoria wrote complaining that Bertie was spending hardly any time with Alix beyond returning every now and then from endless dinner parties and shooting engagements to make her pregnant before disappearing once again.

But for Bertie this double life must have felt like heaven. By refusing to allow him any political role – Queen Victoria barely let Bertie glance at her official papers until 1898 – his mother helped create the playboy she hated. Even when there was a political crisis in which Bertie might have been useful, he was excluded. A massive family row in 1866 based on European political squabbling is a case in point.

Victoria's mad German relations were continually squabbling over Schleswig-Holstein and when Prussia went to war with Austria – a war that ended with Austrian defeat at the Battle of Königgrätz on 3 July 1866 – the family's loyalties were split. It was especially difficult for Alix, several of whose relations had sided with Austria and were subsequently punished by the Prussians. Alix was therefore related to the defeated side and Vicky, Victoria's daughter, had long been married to the Prussian King Fritz. It was a horrible tangle, but despite supporting his wife and her relations, Bertie managed to stay on good terms with his sister Vicky who fully supported the Prussians' punishment of Austria. It was evident that somewhere in Bertie there might well have been a skilful diplomat trying to get out.

Meanwhile in England Bertie enjoyed a brief period of intense popularity, largely as a result of his marriage to Alix and the successful production of an heir. Victoria, on the other hand, had become very unpopular, largely because she insisted on living in a state of almost total seclusion. She had become a recluse and was even booed on one of the few occasions, in 1867, when she agreed to open parliament. A huge crowd dedicated to parliamentary reform had also gathered to protest as she drove past, but reform was a subject about which Victoria cared little. Like her son, she wished only to maintain the status quo.

By the time the future George V was born in June 1865, Alix's increasing deafness and her permanently painful leg had reduced still further the time she and Bertie spent together. By the time their last child, Alexander John, was born in 1871, sexual relations between the couple had become all but impossible. This pushed Bertie further into the arms of his various mistresses. But there is some evidence that for Alix it was a great relief when Bertie decided he no longer wanted to sleep with her. By 1867 she was wearing what was effectively a metal cage around her leg and she was permanently exhausted. Her friend Lady Macclesfield complained that Bertie thought nothing of keeping the Princess up late worrying till he returned from carousing at three in the morning. He rarely told her where he was going or when he would be back and, rather humiliatingly, she had to ask Francis Knollys if he knew.

In this, perhaps the last age of deference to the monarch and the royal family in general, it was still seen as unseemly for anyone to criticise a royal; only socialists and other radicals broke the rules, and they were beyond the pale. Courtiers and advisers, then as now, were sycophantic; they were there to do Bertie's bidding, not to criticise. Only his mother could do that, and she was locked away in her castle at Windsor. The advisers knew their role was to do everything in their power to hide the Prince of Wales's real nature from the public and from the Queen.

In 1867, soon after the birth of Bertie's third child, Louise, he set off for the Continent, ostensibly to visit the Great Exhibition in Paris organised by Napoleon III. The real reason was pleasure away from the prying eyes of the puritanical English.

We don't know exactly what Bertie got up to when he reached Paris that year, but even his ever-faithful secretary Francis Knollys was appalled. Bertie visited the opera and theatre and then went on to dinners that lasted half the night. He insisted his guests should include what even Knollys describes as some of the most notorious prostitutes in Europe.

Later in life Bertie mellowed and in general preferred the company of his mistresses to the more raucous and dangerous atmosphere of the brothel. But a snapshot of the years 1865–85 reveals a man who was what we today would call a sex addict. He was also a nicotine addict and suffered from a serious eating disorder. It wasn't just that he ate vast quantities of food, it was that he ate like a man possessed. It was noted that he scarcely chewed his food in his eagerness to get it down.

Sometime during this visit to Paris, Bertie began affairs with the infamous Giulia Beneni and Hortense Schneider.

Beneni was particularly alluring as she seemed to have absolutely no respect for the fact that he was a Prince. Bertie was delighted by her lack of inhibition, her almost masculine sexual aggression. At a party specially organised for the Prince, she pulled up her skirts and showed him her bare bottom and, when reprimanded by one of the courtiers, she merely laughed and said she thought it a good idea to show the Prince her best feature – and that he needn't worry because she was not going to charge him for the privilege.

Beneni was known as the world's greatest whore – a title in which she delighted – and Bertie visited her whenever he could, no doubt because her sexual talents were unsurpassed, or so it was said.

But there were countless other prostitutes, and the Falstaffian figure of Bertie loved them all – and he invited them to his lavish supper parties.

Another early conquest Bertie managed to fit in between regular visits to Paris was Helen, Lady Forbes, whose daughter, Evie, was almost certainly Bertie's. Bertie always looked after his own and he did as much as he could financially and in other ways for Evie, including agreeing to become godfather to Evie's own son Edward in 1907.

But keeping his aristocratic sexual conquests within a tight social circle could cause complications. In this instance Bertie also slept with Evie's sisters Harriet and Georgiana.

All three sisters were young and beautiful and it is therefore hard to imagine, beyond the lure of power, their interest in the Prince, who was by now very overweight; he also reeked of sweat and tobacco, coughed and wheezed continually and was frequently morose and irritable.

There is no doubt Harriet and Georgiana would have run a mile from a man of Bertie's description had he not been the Prince of

Wales. Of course it helped that Bertie was unfailingly generous with gifts of money and jewels to anyone he could persuade to sleep with him. And it was this generous streak that Alice Keppel above all was able to exploit.

Harriet, Lady Mordaunt, had been Bertie's mistress probably from as early as 1864, and their affair certainly continued after she married in 1866. Her daughter Violet was born in 1869 and was probably Bertie's, though she claimed – loudly and proudly – that Violet was certainly not her husband's but equally certainly that the father could either be Bertie, Lord Cole or Sir Frederick Johnstone.

Bertie always assumed that his aristocratic conquests would be as uncomplicated and undemanding as the prostitutes with whom he slept – he wanted everyone to have fun and then go away quietly if he paid them enough money. He assumed that when he decided to discard them they would simply accept the situation and move on, just as he did. He was like a child, but with terrifying power.

Chapter 8

Secrets and Lies

ERTIE ALWAYS SEEMED surprised when his decision to end a relationship with a mistress led to recriminations. He was even more surprised when one of his mistresses failed to honour the code of silence that dictated you could sleep with as many of your friends' wives as you liked so long as they and their husbands never alluded to what was going on. Most of the time he got away with it, of course.

But filled with a sense of his own power and inviolability, Bertie began to get himself into terrible scrapes. Lady Vane-Tempest, a direct descendant of Charles II's mistress, the much hated Barbara Villiers, became pregnant by Bertie in 1871. She asked for money – a great deal of money – in return for her discretion. Bertie refused, but then spent months terrified she might take her revenge by talking to the press. In the end she disappeared from London and is believed to have had the child in Ramsgate. Lady Vane-Tempest died four years later without ever revealing the sex of the child or what happened to it.

During the 1870s and early 1880s Bertie always conducted several simultaneous affairs. One of these, with Patsy Cornwallis-West, led in 1874 to the birth of her son George.

Bertie had always admired Lady Aylesford, but it was only when she married in 1871 that she became fair game. By the end of that year she was certainly sleeping with the Prince, and the two daughters she gave birth to in the years ahead were believed to have been Bertie's.

Lady Mordaunt, or rather her husband, was the first of his aristocratic mistresses to make a major public fuss. Lord Mordaunt was one of the few aristocrats in Bertie's circle who refused to acquiesce in his wife's adultery with the Prince. When Mordaunt found out what had been going on he was incensed. He sued for divorce, but in a manner that partly paid heed to the rules of the game, he cited Lord Cole and Sir Frederick Johnstone as co-respondents – but not the Prince of Wales. There is no doubt he was furious with Bertie and, all other things being equal, he would probably have dragged the Prince's name into the courts, but all other things were not equal. Bertie ran his relationships and his circle of friends much as a Mafia godfather might run his. The Prince was powerful but he also had powerful friends and Mordaunt was under pressure to keep the Prince out of the whole sordid business. Truth did not matter. Princes were above the law. But in this instance no amount of bullying behind the scenes could keep Bertie entirely out of the case. People quickly became aware that the Prince of Wales was involved. Rumours circulated widely through all classes of society and, as a result, the Prince was finally forced to give evidence when the case came for trial in 1870.

In the witness box Bertie was treated with absurd deference – he was not cross-examined and the judge's summing up was blatantly biased in his favour. Bertie admitted he had visited Lady Mordaunt in her husband's absence on numerous occasions but flatly denied there had been any impropriety. In this he certainly committed perjury, for it was an accepted fact in Victorian England that, in the absence of her husband, a man did not visit a woman to whom he was not married. And throughout Bertie's long philandering career his modus operandi with all his mistresses was to visit them when their husbands were away, just as he had visited Lady Mordaunt. The idea that he visited her while her husband was away simply to enjoy her conversation is preposterous – and it was treated as a joke at the time.

To throw suspicion off Bertie and his circle and to avoid further embarrassment for Lord Mordaunt, a plan was hatched to have Lady Mordaunt declared insane. Officialdom connived in this and poor Lady Mordaunt was duly committed to an asylum. She was to spend the rest of her life – nearly forty years – in various institutions.

She died in 1906. Lord Mordaunt finally divorced her in 1875. Outrageous though this all sounds, it was common in nineteenth-century England. Hundreds of women from all social classes were declared insane simply because, in women, an enthusiasm for sex, especially outside marriage, was seen as a defining characteristic of insanity.

Many years later the Prince's private secretary Francis Knollys revealed that Prime Minister William Gladstone had been involved behind the scenes to protect the Prince. He had made sure the relevant legal professionals and the judiciary were made aware of the outcome to the case required by the royal family and the establishment. They had no interest in finding the truth, but the case revealed that the future Edward VII was a liar and perjurer.

Hard on the heels of his near-disastrous affair with Lady Mordaunt, Bertie became involved with the actress Lillie Langtry. Their affair lasted from 1877 to 1880. In his usual half-witted manner, Bertie thought the affair would never become public and that Langtry's husband would simply accept the situation. However, scandal loomed large once again when a newspaper claimed Bertie was having an affair with Lillie and that her husband planned to sue for divorce naming Bertie as co-respondent. Journalist Adolphus Rosenberg got this bit wrong. Langtry was not planning to divorce his wife, but Bertie *was* having an affair with her. Bertie sued. His solicitor George Lewis would have known that Bertie was lying to the court when he insisted he had never had an affair with the actress. Rosenberg was sentenced to eighteen months in prison. Once again the affair revealed that the future King of England was quite happy to go to almost any lengths to protect his reputation.

Then as now there was, to some extent, one law for the rich and well connected, and another law for everyone else. When Bertie's equerry Lord Somerset was caught in a gay brothel in Cleveland Street, for example, he was allowed to leave the country to escape prosecution. Bertie's eldest son, Albert Victor, Duke of Clarence, was also an enthusiastic visitor to the Cleveland Street brothel. According to Vita Sackville-West, a solicitor was persuaded by the royal family's advisers and the government to commit perjury to ensure no case was ever brought against Albert Victor. So obvious was the lie that the solicitor involved was later struck off. Then, after a suitable lapse of time, a discreet word ensured the solicitor was compensated for what he had done and quietly reinstated. It was a horribly murky business.

But we should perhaps spare a thought for Prince Albert Victor. Known in the family as Eddy, he was certainly homosexual and his early death from pneumonia in 1892 saved the Saxe-Coburgs from the prospect of a gay King. Lord Chief Justice Goddard said at the time: 'It is one of God's mercies that … horrible young man died.'

Having escaped from the Lillie Langtry scandal by the narrowest of margins, Bertie carried on as if nothing had happened, heedless of the advice of Knollys and others. Their advice was not of course that he should lead a better life but that he should be more discreet – they were in effect saying 'do what you like but just don't get caught again'. They would have been delighted if they had known that the wayward Prince was soon to meet a woman who played strictly by the rules, who ensured her husband also played by the rules and who could be guaranteed never to breathe an indiscreet word to anyone. Alice Keppel was to be a godsend to the royal family and the governing classes who, prior to her arrival on the scene, must have been perpetually terrified that Bertie would continue to flounder into embarrassing affairs that would lead to the courts and the whole horrifying business of lying to the public.

❋⟷❋❋⟷❋

Bertie's career as a philanderer probably reached a peak in the 1880s and so many affairs overlapped with each other that it is difficult now to disentangle precisely what was going on. Perhaps most shocking is the fact that Bertie even managed to seduce Lady Churchill, Winston's Churchill's mother, the American Jennie Jerome.

The result of this tangled love life and official secrecy is that it is also all but impossible now to know for certain how many illegitimate children he fathered – a conservative figure would put it at somewhere between six and ten.

But one thing is certain and deeply shocking – in later life Bertie slept with the daughters of women he had seduced as a young man. Some of the daughters may well have been sired by Bertie himself which raises the prospect that Edward VII was involved in incestuous relationships with his own children.

Bertie's affair with Lady Forbes produced, as we have seen, a daughter, christened Evie. Evie in turn gave birth to Audrey and Audrey later became Bertie's mistress. Like a modern day ageing rock star or media mogul, Bertie loved wherever possible to bed women much younger than himself.

In France too Bertie left a trail of illegitimate children. His first aristocratic French mistress was the Princesse de Sagan. Her second son, Paul Louis, born in 1867, was always assumed to be Bertie's. Bertie met the Princess regularly in Paris in the years up to and beyond 1867 and he conducted a simultaneous affair, also in France, with the Comtesse de Pourtalès. Both lived in Paris and Bertie would travel there regularly in disguise using the name 'the Earl of Chester'.

How did Queen Alexandra react to all this? Bertie was considerate to Alix while he was at home, but of course the problem was that he hardly ever was at home and he would accept no challenge to his right to travel widely in England and abroad.

He defended Alix against his mother and agreed with her when their children were named. He also accepted her dislike of his mother's Prussian connections. Bertie's problem was that life with Alix was all about duty – which is why he was only half joking when he described Alix as his brood mare. He described his mistresses and girlfriends, on the other hand, as his 'hacks'; they were designed for an occasional brief, exciting gallop.

Alice Keppel was to become Bertie's ultimate 'hack' – almost literally – if a curious story recounted by the Countess of Athlone is right. In her memoirs the countess recalled that, 'When Uncle Bertie named one of his horses Ecila, everyone knew this transparent disguise was Alice's name in reverse.'

Neglect is the charge most frequently levelled at Bertie when it comes to his wife. And if he was free to do as he pleased, she had no freedom at all. Even if she had wanted to she could not have taken a lover. She was trapped in a gilded cage. And she was married to a man with the immaturity of a child but the appetites of a man. Having grown up without a real childhood Bertie remained childish throughout his adult life. If he couldn't have an extra pudding or cigar or a woman who had taken his fancy, he would rage as he had raged long ago in the schoolroom. No wonder Princess Alexandra gradually retreated into her own private world.

❊⟶❊⟶❊

After surviving by the skin of his teeth the public scandals of his relationships with Lady Mordaunt and Lillie Langtry, Bertie concentrated his sexual interest on the brothels of Paris and on French mistresses who were far enough away to be less likely to cause trouble. His English affairs seemed less troublesome too in the early 1880s, but another crisis was looming. It began when he became entangled with Daisy, Lady Brooke (from 1893 she was Lady Warwick after her husband inherited the earldom). It was to be a relationship that all but destroyed one of his oldest friendships, and not for the first time it made him complicit in illegality.

Daisy Brooke was well known to Bertie and the royal family. Years earlier she had infuriated Queen Victoria by refusing to marry Prince Leopold and had instead married Lord Brooke. Apparently it was a love match. Bertie had been a guest at her wedding.

Like many women saddled with hunting and shooting husbands, Daisy quickly grew bored. She began a long affair with Lord Beresford, who was a member of the Marlborough House set. Daisy eventually gave birth to Beresford's daughter Marjorie, and Lord

Brooke seems to have been unperturbed – so long as he was allowed to continue shooting and hunting, he didn't mind what Daisy got up to. But then something unexpected happened and the Marlborough House set was thrown into chaos.

Beresford told Daisy their affair was over because his wife Mina was pregnant. To Daisy, this seemed a mere pretext and she refused to accept the role of discarded mistress. In her rage she wrote a furious and compromising letter to Lord Beresford telling him he must immediately leave his wife.

Unfortunately for Daisy, Lady Beresford opened the letter and immediately took it to her solicitor. The solicitor wrote to Daisy virtually accusing her of sexual harassment. In a panic and realising that only one man in the country was sufficiently influential to help her, Daisy wrote to Bertie and asked to see him. There is no doubt that Daisy used her charms and hinted strongly to Bertie during her interview with him that she would sleep with him and become his mistress if he would only get her out of the mess she had created.

Dazzled by her good looks and youthful figure, Bertie clearly thought this would be an excellent arrangement. After their interview, he called his carriage and set off for the Beresfords' solicitor George Lewis. What followed would have led to a prison sentence for anyone other than the Prince of Wales. Bertie forced the solicitor to accompany him to the lawyer's office in the city and show him Daisy's original letter. Breaking all the rules that are supposed to govern the legal profession, Lewis did as he was told.

The letter effectively threatened to make the scandal public, so Bertie next visited Lady Beresford and told her that if she did not agree to instruct Lewis to hand over Daisy's original letter, she and her husband would be ostracised. Mina Beresford refused and Bertie was as good as his word. He was always allowed to look through the guest list for any weekend party (or 'Friday to Monday' as it was called) to which he had been invited, and from then on he always crossed through Mina's name. He made doubly sure the Beresfords were hurt by always adding Daisy and her husband to every Friday to Monday party. According to Mina Beresford, the owners of many of the country houses the Prince visited with Daisy in tow were disgusted that he insisted on bringing her but they could do nothing.

The tale took a yet more bizarre turn when Lord Beresford, who we may recall had decided to cast off Daisy after his wife became pregnant, reacted with fury when he discovered that Bertie was now sleeping with her. In a series of interviews Bertie and Beresford bellowed insults at each other. Bertie told Beresford that Daisy no longer wanted him; Beresford claimed it was ungentlemanly to steal another man's mistress.

Having lost their access to the social circles in which they had always moved, the Beresfords were in a difficult position. Mina Beresford took her revenge by helping write a pamphlet about the affair which was circulated in aristocratic circles. Beresford threatened to make the story more widely known, but Bertie was unmoved. Even Bertie's long-suffering wife gave Bertie her full support in the dispute.

Prime Minister Lord Salisbury eventually brokered a deal between the warring parties. If Beresford stopped sending threatening letters, Bertie would send a letter apologising for his part in the affair. The letters were exchanged and a major public scandal averted. But the Beresfords were never really forgiven. They had broken the golden rule of silence and acquiescence. Bertie carried on as before, but his reputation had taken yet another hit and he was beginning to be disliked by some very powerful figures. Lord Salisbury, for example, never invited Bertie to his great house at Hatfield and he made it clear that this was because he despised Bertie's behaviour as both immoral and ungentlemanly.

As Bertie grew older his desire for young mistresses began to be tempered by a desire that they should not only be good-looking – they should also be intelligent and amusing. Unstable characters such as Daisy Brooke and Lady Mordaunt were exciting but dangerous. By the time he met Alice Keppel it was as if he had been primed to respond to her looks and her character – a character already famous for tact, discretion and intelligence.

Bertie's instinct – honed by such near-disasters as the Daisy Brooke affair – began to change; he still made mistakes, but he avoided some of the more highly strung potential mistresses in his circle. In the years that remained before Alice Keppel came along, there were to be other sexual escapades that caused trouble, but never quite on the scale of those of his earlier years.

Meanwhile there were other non-sexual but perhaps equally damaging scandals to deal with.

There is strong circumstantial evidence that Bertie invented an accusation of cheating at cards against Sir William Gordon-Cumming after discovering that Sir William was sleeping with Daisy Brooke.

Gordon-Cumming was descended from one of Britain's most ancient families and was wealthy enough to afford to lose at cards.

He would also have been acutely aware that, for a gentleman, cheating was far more sinful than any amount of sexual misbehaviour.

The cheating incident apparently occurred at Tranby Croft in Yorkshire, the home of Bertie's friend, the ship-owner Arthur Wilson. The other players made Gordon-Cumming sign a paper agreeing never to play cards again or they would make the story public. Gordon-Cumming signed but then sued, and the Prince of Wales found himself giving evidence in court once again. The details became widely known, probably because Daisy Brooke famously could not keep a secret to save her life – she was known as 'babbling Brooke'.

But what made matters worse was that, as in the past, Bertie tried to use his influence to stop the case coming to court. A. N. Wilson points out in his biography of Queen Victoria that rumours were rife that it was actually Bertie who had cheated.

Gordon-Cumming lost his libel case but only because the judge was blatantly biased in his summing up. The jury did as it was told, but outside the court and in the newspapers it was widely believed that Bertie had rigged the whole thing to punish Gordon-Cumming.

Bertie's reputation had taken a further battering because, if nothing else, he had been forced to admit in court that he had been gambling, which was still illegal in Britain.

Radical and even not-so-radical newspapers reported the case and railed against the behaviour of the Prince. Mud began to stick. Having been linked to numerous sexual scandals, Bertie was now found to be a low-life gambler. For many months he was hissed at whenever he appeared in public.

Throughout this period and right up until his relationship with

Alice Keppel began, Bertie pursued his relationship with Daisy Brooke, despite the scandals that swirled around them and despite the fact that Daisy was never quite so keen on the relationship as Bertie was. Like so many of Bertie's mistresses, Daisy – who, unlike Alice Keppel, had no real need of money or gifts – was showered with cash, mostly from money Bertie won at the races. But ultimately, Daisy found Bertie a bore and a slightly disgusting one at that. After their ten years together he was fatter than ever and needed a special apparatus, a bizarre leather harness, to have any hope of copulating with her.

A similar 'lover's seat' festooned with buckles and straps, was frequently shown to visitors to a particular brothel in Paris. It had been made for the notorious Le Chabanais where Bertie regularly availed himself of the services of prostitutes. In any event, by early 1890s sex must have been a struggle, not just for Bertie but also for the women who had to manage his extraordinary bulk.

Daisy Brooke eventually had had enough. Bertie took up almost all her free time and he stank. Long after Bertie died, she confessed that he was also a bore who either groped her a little or simply wanted to sit and look at her. He was also, she said, a spoilt little boy who expected her always to be at his beck and call.

By the mid-1890s Bertie was having electric shock treatment – a favourite Victorian treatment for impotence. But it wasn't enough, and Daisy, always very keen on sex, transferred her affections to a much younger and more vigorous lover, the mine-owner Joseph Laycock.

Bertie was also involved with Jennie Jerome, Lady Churchill (the mother of Winston Churchill). In 1889 Lord Randolph Churchill came home unexpectedly one afternoon and found the Prince with his wife. He asked the Prince to leave, but was too deeply embedded in the establishment world of wife-swapping to make a fuss and, besides, Bertie was by no means his wife's first lover. Indeed, it was widely known that Winston Churchill's brother John had been fathered by Viscount Falmouth. Jennie had a fearsome reputation for promiscuity.

Bertie occasionally escaped the complexities of his relationships with his various mistresses by visiting Rosa Lewis, the eccentric cockney owner of the famous Cavendish Hotel in Jermyn Street. Bertie could stay at the hotel using one of his aliases (probably 'the Earl of Chester') and Rosa would send out into the Haymarket for prostitutes of whom she (and he) approved.

Rosa Lewis's Cavendish was said to be the most entertaining place in London. It even housed a full-blown aristocratic prostitute, who stayed free of charge provided she continued to provide 'gentlemen's services'. If any of Rosa's guests decided not to use her services and instead picked up a girl in Piccadilly without Rosa's permission, Rosa would shout at them when they returned to the hotel: 'We'll get the doctor to look at your winkle in the morning.'

'She always did it when there were others milling about in the hall,' recalled one of her regulars, 'to maximise the embarrassment and teach you never to do it again!'

Curiously Bertie's relationship with Daisy Brooke seems to

have come to an end finally when she became pregnant in 1897. Whether or not the child was Bertie's it is impossible now to say, but it was widely rumoured at the time that he was the father. Princess Alexandra seems to have been particularly upset by Daisy's closeness to Bertie, and the baby was probably the final straw. This was one of the few occasions when Alix completely lost her temper with her errant husband. Bertie's reaction was simply to point out that if she made a fuss it would merely result in a visit to the divorce courts. Alix backed down and Bertie's baby with Daisy was born in March 1898. Daisy told everyone that Bertie was not the father but few believed her.

Bertie and Daisy remained friends, but perhaps shaken by Alix's rage over the pregnancy of his long-term mistress, Bertie began to look elsewhere and in the early part of 1898 he met the woman who was to dominate the rest of his life. Though he was still to visit prostitutes – where, as he grew older, he preferred to watch others having sex – Bertie was almost instantly besotted by Alice Keppel.

The word 'mistress', which is almost exclusively used to describe aristocratic women who sleep with wealthy men for money, includes a suggestion that an aristocratic mistress offers more than just sex – and in Alice Keppel's case this was certainly true. She offered intelligence, humour and an uncanny ability to prevent the Prince becoming bored and irritable, which might happen at a moment's notice if the Marlborough House set (or anyone else) failed to put itself out to entertain him.

Of course middle-class and working-class mistresses might be just as likely to offer interesting and amusing conversation, but convention demands that upper-class women should somehow be seen in a different light. Certainly Bertie's later mistresses, especially Alice Keppel, were chosen in a different way from the earlier ones where good looks and sexual appeal always trumped intelligence and discretion. Bertie would have sensed that in Alice Keppel he had found a woman who combined the looks upon which he insisted with mental capacities that had been lacking in many of his earlier conquests. Bertie would have known that this wonderfully attractive woman would never break the code of the aristocracy. She would keep her affairs – including her affair with him – to herself. But what she may not have made quite so clear to him is that she would only do it if she was very handsomely paid.

As we have seen, she used her relationship with Bertie ruthlessly, to make herself one of the richest women in Britain. And the money she gained from her affair with Bertie and indeed from her earlier lovers was handed on to her daughters and granddaughters. It was money from which Camilla, the present Duchess of Cornwall, benefited before her marriage to her long-term lover Prince Charles.

Chapter 9

La Favourite

ALICE HAD BEEN married for seven years by the time she met Bertie. Her affairs with bank managers and other aristocrats had swelled the family coffers, but Alice wanted to be draped in the finest furs and pearls; she wanted to entertain in the grandest possible fashion and she knew that the best route to that kind of life was via Bertie's weakness for large-breasted, vaguely masculine women.

That night in 1898 when they met at Lady Howe's and spent the evening sitting at the top of a flight of steps would have been a godsend for Alice. She knew the sort of lifestyle the Prince enjoyed and how much it cost. For a gold-digging fortune-hunter like Alice, Bertie was the mother lode.

But how was Bertie able to fund his own lavish lifestyle as well as making Alice Keppel a multi-millionairess? To find out we need to look at Bertie's manipulation of Britain's wealthy Jews.

❋⚬━❋❋━⚬❋

Bertie's annual income was well over £100,000, but throughout his years as Prince of Wales he overspent by as much as £40,000 a year. The government and his advisers tried to control this profligacy but Bertie hated the idea of his expenditure being minutely examined by Parliament, which is what would have happened if he had asked for an increase in his allowance. To get round this he befriended a number of wealthy Jews who were desperate to find a place in society. They were expected to invest Bertie's money profitably; in return they would be invited into the notoriously anti-Semitic world of the English upper classes.

Various biographers and historians have commented on Bertie's lack of prejudice against Jews and it is certainly true that his attitudes stand out when compared to the attitudes of his contemporaries. Anti-Semitism was simply the norm in England in the late nineteenth century and well into the twentieth century. However commercially successful British Jews became they were always viewed with distaste by the English governing class. As late as the 1930s

Virginia Woolf, who was married to a Jew, still writes disparagingly about Jews in her letters. This was typical, but any credit Bertie might be given for his enlightened attitudes needs to be seen alongside his desperate desire to be allowed to spend as he pleased. Bertie would not have befriended the various Jews he introduced into society if they had not been willing to lend him very large sums of money.

It all began with a loan of £60,000 from his old friend Natty Rothschild, money that was never paid back. Later Baron Hirsch funded Bertie through the 1890s, probably to the tune of at least £300,000 – perhaps £15 million in today's values. Hirsch never asked for the money back, but in return for his financial support he was pushed into society. Though Bertie's friends hated inviting Hirsch to their houses, they had to do it as Bertie insisted. They were quite open about their dislike of his new friends. Lord Derby, for example, wrote that Hirsch, being Jewish, could not be a gentleman and was probably not honest. In nineteenth-century England no Jew was ever seen as honest.

After Hirsch died in 1896 Bertie quickly latched on to another wealthy Jew, Ernest Cassel. So desperate was Cassel for social acceptance that he agreed to manage Bertie's money, giving Bertie any profits while absorbing any losses himself. Cassel's need to identify with the Prince reached such a peak that he even began to trim his beard so that it looked like Bertie's; he hung a portrait of the Prince in his Park Lane mansion and made Bertie very rich indeed. And as Bertie became ever-richer through the late 1890s and early 1900s, so he in turn made Alice Keppel very rich. Not only did Bertie heap presents of cash and jewels on Alice but he also found a job for her husband – a job that was well paid but involved little or no work – and for her ever-present brother Archie who became groom-in-waiting to Edward from 1907 to 1910.

The story that Alice and Bertie sat at the top of the steps of Lady Howe's house engrossed in each other for two hours may be apocryphal, but the fact that the story gained currency says something about the speed with which Alice Keppel supplanted Daisy Brooke. It was as if, having given up Daisy, Bertie was immediately open to offers. He could not bear to be without a new mistress for long.

In 1898 Alice was twenty-nine, dazzlingly good-looking and famously witty. Bertie was fifty-seven, grossly overweight, malodorous and asthmatic. Whatever her faults – her love of money, her profound hypocrisy and her ruthlessness – she had one additional quality that no one has ever disputed. She was a brilliant talker who could be very funny hour after hour without flagging and without indulging in malicious gossip. It was often said of her that she never spoke ill of anyone and that when she set out to captivate she was almost always successful.

In his autobiography *Left Hand, Right Hand!*, published in 1948, just a year after Alice died, Osbert Sitwell remembered visits to the Keppel's London house. He wrote:

> ...the hostess [Alice Keppel] conducted the running of her house as a
> work of art ... I liked greatly to listen to her talking: if it were possible

to lure her away from the bridge table she would remove from her mouth for a moment the cigarette which she would be smoking with an air of determination, through a long holder, and turn upon the person to whom she was speaking her large humorous, kindly, peculiarly discerning eyes. Her conversation was lit by humour, insight and the utmost good nature … moreover, a vein of fantasy, a power of enchantment would often lift what she was saying … her talk had a boldness about it, an absence of all pettiness that helped to make her a memorable figure.

Though credited with having a benign influence on Bertie, she was not universally popular. Princess Alexandra's friends and family certainly disliked her. In 1902 Princess Mary, the wife of the future George V, wrote to a friend from Cowes on the Isle of Wight to say how furious she thought Alix would be when Mrs Keppel joined the party. Prince George himself wrote: 'Mrs Keppel arrives tomorrow … peace and quiet will not remain.'

Prince George (later George V) had inherited his grandfather Albert's seriousness and strictness. Throughout his life he could not bear to hear Alice's name mentioned and she is almost never mentioned in the memoirs of royal aides or hangers-on. The truth is that George V was horribly embarrassed by his father's decades of philandering. He believed, as his grandmother and grandfather had believed, that the royal family should be a moral exemplum for the nation.

One member of the royal family who did recall Mrs Keppel was Princess Alice, Duchess of Gloucester, wife of Henry, the third son of George V. Writing in old age she said that Mrs Keppel 'never flaunted herself or took advantage of her position as the King's favourite'. But Alice's memoirs are typically anodyne – she wanted life as she had known it as a young woman to be remembered as civilised and decorous, a world where scandal simply did not exist.

Viscount Esher, who knew Alice Keppel well, took a very different view. He disliked her intensely. He wrote that he thought she was simply a liar. He also recalled that Queen Alexandra hated the sight of Alice but felt powerless to do anything about her.

Alice was jealous of those who competed with her and was disliked by Bertie's other confidantes, but she used her jealousy skilfully to stimulate Bertie's desire for her. She was careful never to become angry with him but rather to cajole and merely hint at her feelings. Alice seems to have worried unduly about Agnes Keyser, a mistress whom Bertie relied on entirely for mothering rather than sex. Keyser lived near Alice Keppel's old home near Belgrave Square and spent her time doing what the Victorians called 'good works'. In the First World War she ran a hospital for injured officers. Keyser was scarcely a serious romantic rival, but Bertie liked to bounce continually from one mistress to another and then back again simply to stave off boredom.

Alice knew that she was not universally admired but she didn't care. Some members of the royal family and courtiers hated her but she enjoyed her power while it lasted and knew that while Bertie lived her enemies were largely powerless. She would have hated to be seen as a prostitute and in truth felt she was far more even than a mistress. In later life she gave friends the impression she felt she was Bertie's 'real' wife. In photos of Bertie at Friday to Monday parties at grand houses, Alice is nearly always there, but rarely next to Bertie; always ready when he needed her but at a discreet distance.

❈──❈❈──❈

Bertie no doubt loved Alice or at least could never do without her. One of the things about her he seems to have liked best was her sartorial skill. He was obsessed with the idea that people should dress not only correctly but also magnificently. Alice was acutely aware of this and dressed accordingly. She wore the finest silk and was invariably festooned with pearls and diamonds. She would spend more than half the day getting ready for any social engagement, as Agnes Cook recalled:

> You have to remember that this was in the days before casual clothes and things such as zips! It was also a time when to create the right sort of shape and appearance a society woman like Mrs Keppel had to wear many layers and each layer had to be fitted exactly one above the other by her lady's maid – once buttoned into her various dresses and under-dresses Alice couldn't get out without help. Then on top of the dresses went layers and layers of jewellery, brooches, bits of silk and all sorts of oddments. The more the better. It wasn't considered vulgar at all, all this showy behaviour – it was more that you were proving to everyone that you owned masses of the best things and you had enough money to spend all day getting into them.

Bertie loved all this and loved the fact that Alice never got it wrong

– unlike Consuelo, Duchess of Marlborough, who Bertie rudely upbraided in front of his assembled guests because she was wearing a diamond crescent hair band instead of a proper tiara. But this obsession with trivia is perhaps not surprising given that Bertie spent most of his life until he became King at sixty with nothing serious to do. Kept out of everything concerning government by his mother, Bertie was an old man when the chance for a serious role became possible, but it had all come too late, as he said himself.

Bertie established the modern idea of the British monarch as someone good at opening fêtes and new buildings, launching ships and asking people if they had come far – but it was a role he adopted out of sheer necessity. When he became King he was tired and old and fixed in his habits. He tried to deal with government papers but work exhausted him and he was only ever partially successful. Instead he quietly allowed professional politicians to do all the real work, and that tradition has continued to this day. We like the modern monarchy because, in the political sense, it does as it is told. If Queen Victoria didn't like the political complexion of a particular government she refused to open parliament. Can anyone really imagine a modern monarch refusing to open parliament in the same way simply because she disliked the new Prime Minister? It is unimaginable and it is this royal separation from politics that began in its modern form with Bertie. He signed more papers, it is true, after becoming King, but he found politics boring; he put his energies into his private life and into the business of being seen and adding his name to charitable organisations. He liked ceremony and the sound of cheering crowds. He even revived a long vanished tradition – that women should kiss a King's hand when they were introduced.

Having been bullied he knew how to bully and would often humiliate his courtiers – no one was allowed to go to bed before he did and he liked to stay up late. On one occasion in the early hours of the morning he sent a servant to wake the 75-year-old courtier Sir Dighton Probyn. Probyn, unwell and exhausted, had sneaked off to bed without permission and Bertie wanted him back.

Two things reveal the huge change that came over the monarchy when Queen Victoria died in 1901. First Edward insisted on a lavish opening of parliament at which he presided, dressed in full regalia and having brought the state coach out of retirement so he could be seen on his journey to Westminster. His mother would have been horrified.

The second relates to the first in that Bertie invited virtually all his women friends – including current and former mistresses – to the ceremony. He wanted to show off in front of them and now that his time had arrived he wanted the emphasis to be on his status as King rather than his qualities as a man. He knew he had few qualities as a man so if he was to get the recognition he felt he deserved he had to get it through pomp and ceremony and being seen in public.

His mother had been a virtual recluse for nearly forty years. She hardly ever opened parliament and when she did someone else made her speech. Bertie changed all that. And at the various houses and palaces where his mother's tastes had dominated life he changed everything. He got rid of her favourite Indian retainers, threw out her letters and redecorated the rooms she had kept unchanged for decades.

Curiously, Victoria had combined reclusiveness with a desire to let people know how she felt – she published her diaries under the title *Leaves from the Journal of our Life in the Highlands*. Dull reading for the most part, the book does hint at barely concealed passions. Bertie was having none of this. The public persona was all the public was going to get from him, which is why those diaries of his that have survived reveal only the times and dates of various meetings. Where he is planning to meet a mistress, the diaries include initials and a time. And that's it.

Now that Bertie was King, no one was going to control whom he saw or what he did. His gambling and womanising were to continue until the end of his life and his one sorrow was that his physical health declined rapidly after he finally took over from his mother.

Central to his short reign was Alice Keppel. She had been vital to him from that first meeting in 1898 and she was to remain so until he died.

Most historians agree that George and Alice Keppel had stopped having sex within a year or two of their marriage, but amid endless speculation about the paternity of Alice's first child, Violet, the possibly scandalous paternity of her second child has been forgotten.

No one seriously believes that Violet Keppel, who was to enjoy a scandalous liaison with the writer Victoria Sackville-West, was George Keppel's daughter. It was generally accepted and never contradicted by Alice herself that Violet was, as we have seen, the daughter of banker Ernest Beckett.

In return for her sexual services, Beckett added tens of thousands of pounds to Alice's fortune and, having showered her with money, Beckett then helped her invest very wisely. Her growing capital, increasingly invested in railway stock, began to earn large amounts of interest. The money more than compensated for any rumours that Violet was illegitimate.

And Alice's vastly increased wealth meant that her husband George and brother Archie were able to live a life of extraordinary luxury. Agnes Cook never forgot her mother's stories from this period in Alice's life:

Well, the servant gossip at the time was that Mrs Keppel set aside two, sometimes three afternoons a week for her gentlemen visitors, even after she had taken up with the Prince of Wales. She always saw them in the afternoon because it took her all morning to have a bath and get dressed. The servants were amazed that she bothered with some of her gentlemen visitors. She can't have been letting them have her because they were good-looking because they weren't.

None was as handsome as her husband but then the servants knew he never slept with Alice. Their relationship consisted of nodding at each other when they passed each other on the stairs.

George liked to meet his lady friends in the afternoon when Alice met the King or her other admirers. He liked young actresses and the young wives of his acquaintances but he was so scrupulously and obsessively tidy that he rarely saw these women at home.

According to my mother Alice did change after Bertie became King. She saw her other men less frequently for a while but never quite gave them up.

But if Alice was still seeing other men she was discreet about it and would have ensured that Bertie did not know. One of the curiosities about Bertie was that he didn't mind his mistresses sleeping with their husbands, but hated it if they had other lovers. Bertie of course was far more useful than any of her earlier lovers had been, but her association with him came at a price because she loved sex and Bertie was increasingly unable to provide it. And there were other difficulties.

The devoutly Catholic Duke of Norfolk refused absolutely to invite Alice to his house, even at the height of her influence and power. Lord Salisbury, as we have seen, took a similar view and never invited her to Hatfield House. Alice was seen as immoral by the religious, and grasping and manipulative by secular critics. But even her harshest critics tended to be dazzled by her charm when and if they actually met her.

Virginia Woolf, who met Alice in old age, was, as we have also seen, characteristically unkind, describing her as 'swarthy, thick-set, raddled and short'. She damned Alice as an 'old grasper whose fists have been in the moneybags these fifty years'. Alice's love of money and her determination to get as much of it as possible had clearly become legendary by the time Woolf wrote her diary entry in 1932.

Other scraps fill out a less than flattering picture. Alice herself joked that Queen Alexandra was relieved that Bertie took Alice and his other mistresses to bed as it meant she didn't have to sleep with him.

Like Daisy Warwick and so many of Bertie's other mistresses, Alice saw the Prince as a means to an end, but she also loved the glamour of associating with him. As his favoured mistress she knew she would be treated by most people almost as if she were Queen – when the couple attended the theatre the crowds would shout for Alice not Alix and, with the few exceptions mentioned, even the most censorious of Bertie's friends would not be able to refuse to invite her to their houses if Bertie insisted on it.

Being Bertie's mistress was to exist at the highest levels of luxury and influence – levels Alice could not have hoped to attain as George's Keppel's wife.

Soon after Alice and Bertie consummated their relationship, Alice and her husband would have discussed this latest conquest because the financial and social implications for them both were hugely significant. George no doubt loved the fact that, while playing the part of the aristocratic family man, beautifully dressed, leisurely in his pursuits and able to spend money as if it would never run out, he could rely on his wife to keep the necessary funds coming in.

George was such an incompetent that by the early 1890s he had been involved in three failed businesses. He liked to think he was an intelligent man who deserved employment that was in keeping with his sense of his own worth, but everything he touched fell apart.

Alice asked Bertie if he could do anything for George and Bertie duly obliged. Indeed, he solved two problems in one go. In order to keep George away during the day when Bertie liked to visit Alice he persuaded his friend, the tea merchant Sir Thomas Lipton, to give George a job that might be seen as prestigious but actually involved almost no work. The job was virtually a sinecure. George was supposed to try to drum up business for the firm by using his influence, but in all the years he worked for Lipton it seems he generated no business at all. The other great advantage of finding George a job was that it was another means by which Bertie could direct money to Mrs Keppel. If George had plenty of money from Lipton, then Alice could invest everything she received from Bertie.

The deal was that in return for his generosity to herself, George and Archie, Alice Keppel would never betray Bertie's secrets; never complain if and when he slept with other women; never make demands other than financial ones. She would always be available to him, never creating difficulties and always ready to soothe and amuse, rather like the infinitely tolerant, infinitely indulgent mother he never had.

From the time Bertie met Alice until he died in 1910, Bertie seems to have lost whatever hold he may once have had on Queen Alexandra. Marginalised and deeply upset by his promiscuity, she spent more and more time away visiting her relatives in Denmark. It must have seemed ironic to Alix that the only time Bertie seemed to want to pay her any attention was when she was away on these trips. Then he would write to her every day, and when a visit to Denmark at the end of 1898 was prolonged after the Queen of Denmark's death, Bertie became irritable when she ignored his letters.

But generally, now that she had stopped being his 'brood mare', Alix was irrelevant. Bertie simply had no time for a woman who wanted a quiet life; he was baffled and hurt that she disliked the company of his women friends such as Alice Keppel. In her absence Bertie twisted things in his own mind until he was convinced he was being neglected by Alix. He wrote to his son George, the future George V, complaining that Alix 'kept him in the dark'.

Alice lit up the last decade of Bertie's life but almost as soon as he met her he began to suffer bouts of serious ill health. The year 1898 was a bad one for Bertie. He fell over and fractured his leg and then developed pleurisy. Illness and recuperation especially made him more irritable than usual because his only interests involved the things that made him ill – shooting pheasants in winter, playing cards, staying up late, overeating, drinking and smoking. His doctors insisted on rest and Bertie hated it, but Alice Keppel was always there to soothe and entertain.

Other friends who became more important as the 1890s drew to a close were the Portuguese diplomat the Marquis de Soveral (also known as the Blue Monkey) and Bertie's ever-reliable financier Ernest Cassel. De Soveral didn't provide money but he was very good at making Bertie laugh and, almost uniquely among Bertie's friends, he was greatly liked by Alix. There is little doubt that de Soveral helped smooth relations between Bertie and Alix on many occasions. This inner circle of friends met regularly at Sandringham and Marlborough House, but Mr and Mrs George Keppel never received a joint invitation. The proprieties were still there to be observed, however, so Bertie always sent individual invitations – one to George and another to Alice. It was Bertie's way of signalling that Alice could come if George could not. George always knew he could not.

Alice Keppel, de Soveral and Cassel were the three most important figures in the last fifteen years of Bertie's life. There were always sexual encounters in addition to those with Alice, but none became central to Bertie's life – with perhaps one exception: Agnes Keyser.

Though Bertie enjoyed some sort of physical relationship with Agnes at the start of their relationship, he seems mostly to have visited her because she was strict with him; she made him eat plain food and go to bed early. She gently scolded him and fussed over him like a mother hen, which made him laugh. She was enormously concerned for his welfare but did not indulge his every whim as his other mistresses invariably did. Agnes saw Bertie as someone who needed looking after, and every now and then Bertie agreed with her. It was as if both Alice and Agnes provided sex but also two sides of a maternal personality – one indulgent, the other strict but caring.

Chapter 10

King at Last

B Y THE WINTER of 1900 it was clear that the ultimate controlling figure in Bertie's life was dying. His mother had developed dementia and rapidly began to decline physically. By January 1901 she was dead and the event for which Bertie had waited his whole life had at last come to pass. He was King. Overnight he went from being treated, at his mother's insistence, as someone who could not be trusted even to look at official papers, to someone bombarded with memos and letters, official requests, policy papers and all the paraphernalia of government.

Bertie immediately became depressed. He told Alix that it had all come too late and there is no doubt he felt his reputation as a glutton and philanderer made people think he was simply not up to the job of being King. Having been excluded for so long his instinct was probably right: he was not up to the job, but with Alice Keppel's help he got round the problem by re-inventing the role of King; where his mother had wanted political influence, he accepted he could have none, but he would make up for it by being highly visible where she had been invisible.

Knowing that it could not be long before Bertie became King, Alice and George had moved to suitably grand accommodation. In 1899, two years before the old Queen's death, they bought their lease on 30 Portman Square. They took with them their ever-growing team of servants, including Agnes Cook's mother. Agnes recalled:

> My mother always said that even the servants felt they'd had a sort of promotion along with the family, but however stupid the Keppels thought their servants were, they must have known really that the servants as much as anyone else knew that Alice had insisted on and paid for the move just to be closer to Marlborough House and Buckingham Palace.

> The bills to run the new house, which was actually almost as grand

as Marlborough House itself, would have been colossal, but my mother and everyone else knew that the person footing the bills was Bertie. Mrs Keppel was apparently brilliant and subtle at hinting to Bertie that life would be so much brighter for them both if only the house could be redecorated or if more servants could be there so that they could enjoy themselves without her having to worry about what was going on below stairs. She would never have asked outright for money, she was far too clever for that – she would have presented a need that, if met, would make Bertie's life more fun. And to be fair to Bertie he was by all accounts immensely generous – the heaps of flowers and furniture and jewels that constantly arrived for Alice were amazing.

By the time Bertie became King, Alice and even occasionally George were regular visitors to Sandringham where Bertie had always been able to indulge his eccentricities. One of his madder ideas was that guests should be weighed when they arrived and then weighed again when they left. No doubt he hoped that lavish dining would ensure that at least one or two of his guests might eventually be as overweight as he was.

By the autumn of 1899 Alice was pregnant. This was a huge shock and London society buzzed with rumours of who the father might be. It was widely known that George Keppel had long ago ceased to share his wife's bed, and though Alice was reputed to be sexually rapacious, it was assumed by those in her inner circle that Bertie was the father. During the first few months of her liaison with Bertie, Alice was still sleeping with at least two other men, but according to the servants at least, she was only sleeping with Bertie at the time she became pregnant.

Agnes recalls her mother's excitement at the news:

Down in the servants' hall it was the only subject of conversation for weeks. My mother always said that it was understood and accepted by all the servants that Mrs Keppel was going to have a child and that that child's father was the Prince of Wales. It was obvious because the two of them had been at it like rabbits for months, although the joke was that Bertie was so fat that poor Mrs Keppel had had to do all the work!

In later years I was always amazed that this obvious fact – that Mrs Keppel's second child, the great-grandmother of Camilla Parker Bowles, was possibly the King's child – was never mentioned. It was as if there was a conspiracy of silence. And I was deeply shocked, but not at all surprised, when I read in the newspapers that Camilla Parker Bowles and Charles were sleeping together – I knew they were effectively cousins but no one else ever seemed to mention it.

That was when I realised it had been forgotten (or suppressed) by everyone, except a few former servants like me who were still alive and whose families had worked for the Keppels.

Bertie might have been slowing down a bit sexually when he met Mrs Keppel, but he wasn't quite past it by the late 1890s. She was his last really big fling. He was occasionally ill then it is true, but it was only a few years after he became King that he started to be ill almost continually. Up to about 1900 and well into Mrs Keppel's pregnancy, he was still paying regular visits to her and I can tell you for a fact

– or at least what my mother called a fact – that he was still sleeping with her. The truth is Bertie was still reasonably vigorous at this time and he had a real passion for Alice – he was really excited by the fact that *she* was really excited by sex. Us cockney girls used to say she was a right dirty bird!

My mother always said that the aristocracy and upper classes were disgusting. She used to make a joke that they'd had so many advantages in life that they had no idea how to behave and we should feel sorry for them. She used to say, 'Poor Mrs Keppel didn't realise that it was wrong to sleep with lots of men at the same time. She had no idea you were supposed to sleep with your husband.' Of course she was teasing but there was some truth in what she said. The governing classes then and probably now as well feel that different rules apply to them – they can tell us to be moral but don't have to be moral themselves. They tell us to pay our taxes and not break the law but avoid taxes and break the law themselves because they can get away with it. My mother's favourite phrase was to say the Keppels and others like them 'haven't had the advantages of our disadvantages'!

My mother said the servants used to make a bit of a joke of Bertie's visits to Mrs Keppel. They would try to find a reason to walk along the corridor outside her rooms and try to hear Bertie puffing and blowing like an old steam engine.

Agnes Cook's memories bring to light a scandalous possibility: that the child born to Alice in 1900 was the Prince of Wales's daughter. She was named Sonia.

Almost a century later, Sonia's granddaughter would follow in a grand tradition of royal mistresses when she became the lover of Charles, another Prince of Wales. If Sonia was indeed the Prince's daughter, then Charles and Camilla were not only repeating history when they began their love affair; they would also have been blood relatives.

Agnes Cook again:

> Oh, there was no doubt among the servants because how could there be? All the dates add up and we all thought Mrs Keppel wanted to have a child by the man who was soon to be King – it was a good way of binding him to her.
>
> After about 1903 or 1904 Bertie was so fat and ill that he couldn't do much other than sit on the sofa and hold Mrs Keppel's hand, but that was enough for him. He and Mrs Keppel now had Sonia to think about.
>
> As Bertie lost interest in having sex with Alice she started having sex again with other men but she was careful to make sure it wasn't too obvious to Bertie. The point is that well into middle age Alice couldn't do without sex.

On the day Sonia was born, 24 May 1900, the big house in Portman Square was filled with flowers, and most of them came from Bertie – he was too discreet to turn up in person but his coach arrived packed to overflowing with Alice's favourite blooms, but also with *his* favourite (and distinctive) yellow roses.

We may be shocked now that Charles, Prince of Wales and his wife Camilla could be blood relatives, but at the time of Sonia's birth her paternity was taken for granted by those who knew Mrs Keppel. At the age of four she looked just like the King – her likeness to him was frequently noted and it was confirmed by her extraordinary likeness, when she was still a toddler, to a small portrait of Bertie made in 1843 when he was two by court painter William Ross.

Sonia's sister, Violet, knew she was Beckett's daughter and she hated it. She didn't mind that George was not her father, but all her life she fantasised that Edward VII was her father and in her old age she would insist again and again to anyone who would listen that she, rather than Sonia, was the child of a King. It clearly rankled that privately Sonia had always been known as the King's child and Violet was simply jealous. Why have a bank manager for a father when you could claim a King?

Bertie's reputation was now so fixed and his relationship with Alice so widely known, that it would have been more of a surprise if he had not been the father of Sonia Keppel. Society gossips referred to Sonia as another 'FitzEdward'. In earlier centuries the prefix 'Fitz' meant the holder of the name was illegitimate.

After Sonia, Alice and Bertie's relationship settled into the calm of a long, steady union; Alice was happy to provide the King with as much hand-holding as he needed, provided he continued to supply her with money and jewels. But away from Bertie and without his knowledge, she was soon sleeping once again with her fellow Portman Square resident and long-term lover, Lord Alington. And in the years ahead there were to be many others.

So little was known a century and more ago about the effects of obesity and smoking that Edward probably had no real idea his increasing impotence was the result of his lifestyle rather than anything else. As we have seen, he tried to restore his sexual prowess with electrotherapy but inevitably the treatment failed. According to Agnes Cook this upset the King deeply. It also made him angry:

> My mother said the King was heard weeping one day in Mrs Keppel's drawing room – he had failed once again to have sex with her. It was a few weeks after this that her lady's maid found what today would be called a sex aid in Mrs Keppel's bedroom – they were common at the time but were advertised in magazines as 'female tension relievers'. There was a pretence that they had nothing to do with sex. But they were sex toys designed to help women achieve orgasm. Mrs Keppel certainly had one.

Such devices were commonly used by upper-class women who could afford them. Rose Plummer, who worked in a grand house in London in the 1920s, recalled finding something similar in her mistress's bag:

> While I was hanging up her clothes she went into her adjoining sitting room and I emptied her bag. Now you'll never believe this, but she had a sex aid in there. She must have known I'd find it. I didn't know it was a sex aid at the time but I found out later. They were very common and doctors used to suggest women buy them to stop

them being neurotic. Most of the women who bought them probably didn't think they had anything to do with sex either! In the late 1930s a friend of mine went to her doctor to ask if there was anything wrong because she didn't enjoy sex with her husband. The doctor said, 'Do you want people to think you are a prostitute?' Loads of people thought that only prostitutes liked sex.

Anyway, these tension relievers were for posh women who got sexually frustrated – they bought a little device to sort themselves out! It was an old-fashioned vibrator!

Alice's interest in Bertie was mostly to do with money and position, so she worried when he was ill. If and when he died, her perks would vanish overnight. She knew she would be shunned by many of those closest to the King and many of the great houses where she had formerly been welcome would shut their doors in her face. Every bout of flu, every asthma attack filled Alice with dread, and there were signs already that he was physically fragile. During a visit to the Rothschild's house at Waddesdon in Buckinghamshire in 1898 he had fallen badly and fractured a leg. Shocked and worried by the dramatic effect a relatively minor injury had on the King, Alice immediately wrote to the Marquis de Soveral begging him to intervene, to try to persuade Bertie to see a proper doctor.

A few years later she almost fainted when Bertie telegraphed to say that during a train journey through France a young man had poked a gun through the carriage window and fired a shot at

Bertie. Luckily it missed and the fifteen-year-old would-be assassin was overpowered before he could fire again. This combined with Bertie's increasing bulk and refusal to eat less made Alice permanently concerned. She hated the idea of losing him. No one would argue that she loved him but, more importantly, she revelled in her status as first mistress; she loved the invitations; the grovelling of assistants at Duveen the antiques dealers and at diamond merchants Tiffany, at Worth and other dressmakers; but best of all she loved the enormous wealth that she had managed to build up.

No one knows now exactly how rich she eventually became, but some idea of her fortune can be gained from the fact that, as we have seen, for many years before and after the Second World War she paid for a suite of rooms to be kept permanently available at the Ritz for her by then only occasional visits to London.

<hr />

Despite his own unorthodox personal relationships, Bertie seems to have had a particular hatred for what might best be called his mother's more eccentric friends. He took a delight in destroying as many as possible of the physical reminders – photos and mementoes – of his mother's links with John Brown and the Munshi, her favourite Indian servant.

It was as if Bertie suspected his mother had been too close to these men – and there is some evidence that Victoria's relationship with John Brown may indeed have had a sexual element. But Bertie's reaction was about anger and revenge, not love.

He tried to give the impression that he was deeply upset by his mother's death and would not therefore be enjoying the usual social round, but it was all pretence and he could only keep it up for a few weeks. He avoided public places where he might leave himself open to criticism, but his private gambling and elaborate dinners continued as if nothing had happened.

If the psychologists are right and overeating is a form of violence against one's self, then Bertie's self-hatred became, if anything, worse after the death of his mother. He ate and drank more than ever and seemed hardly to care, at times, whether he lived or died.

Agnes Cook recalled the level of worry about the King in the Keppel household:

> My mother told me that at times the whole house talked of nothing but the King's health. Mrs Keppel knew he was eating and smoking himself to death but she was too careful and subtle to try to change his behaviour directly – he delighted in her company because she never told him what to do and she wasn't going to risk her relationship with him even to save his life.
>
> The butler, footmen and various maids who overheard the Keppels' conversations about the King always brought the gossip down to the servants' hall. It was clear that both George and Alice Keppel were worried about what they would do if and when the King died. By 1905 or 1906 Alice was often in tears at the thought that she might suddenly find herself out in the cold as it were. She knew that Bertie was slowly but surely killing himself and that he probably wanted to do it.

Alice Keppel was a very shrewd woman. With Bertie dead her enemies would all pounce. She knew Queen Alexandra and her children,
including the future George V, could not stand the sight of her. Alice
wanted to stop the King killing himself but she knew he did not want
to live if living meant moderating his eating, drinking and smoking.

Publicly of course Alice was all smiles. She went everywhere with
Bertie now that he was King and there was no one left who would
dare criticise him openly. Even the newspapers of the time commented that the King's real companion was not the Queen but *la
favourite*. In fact, Alice was the woman he should have married;
Alice was probably the woman he *would* have married if the royal
family had not been so foolish as to put dynastic considerations
before personal happiness. And he was fierce in her defence. He
even liked to tease people who he knew would object to Alice – on
one occasion he deliberately placed her next to the Archbishop of
Canterbury at dinner. Within minutes of sitting down she apparently had him eating out of her hand.

Alice sensed in an instant when Bertie was bored and she would
adjust her conversation to ensure that boredom was always kept at
bay. Her almost permanent good temper was even noticed by the
servants, as Agnes Cook recalled:

My mother said that Mrs Keppel was unusual among employers at
that time in that she might ask after one of the maids who was ill.
This was almost shocking as many employers who liked to think
of themselves as decent and humane, would not think twice about

sacking a servant who could not work through sickness. Mrs Keppel was slightly different, perhaps because she knew that the servants by now knew many of her most intimate secrets. And later in her life she even paid a little above the going rate! Her insistence on sacking servants who got pregnant had little to do with morality and every-thing to do with ensuring that the public face of her household was as respectable as possible. This was essential because rumours about her own behaviour were widespread and she didn't want that situa-tion made worse by gossip about her servants. It was all part of her instinct for survival.

Various diaries of the time, including that written by Bertie's inti-mate friend Lord Carrington, attest to the intensity from 1901 of the King's feelings, but Carrington did not approve of what seemed to him and other courtiers a dangerous obsession. He confided acidly to his diary, 'Mrs Keppel is in high favour'.

The King's 'little dinners with Mrs George' were widely dis-cussed at court but not mentioned more widely in the establishment newspapers of the time. This was less true of the increasing num-ber of radical newspapers. *The Clarion*, for example, regularly published criticisms of the King's character and lifestyle. In one article he is described as 'Pleasure loving, embarrassing, and openly contemptuous'.

Bertie was more sensitive to public criticism now than he had been as Prince of Wales. He was persuaded, by Alice Keppel and others, to drop his old friend and mistress Daisy Brooke when she eventually did speak to the newspapers. Bertie even began to behave in ways that were reminiscent of his mother. Just as Bertie had been kept well away from power by his mother, so too Queen Alexandra was kept away from the duties of a Queen by Bertie, who insisted on doing everything himself, even to the point of breaking with protocol.

As she was rarely included in official engagements, Alix seems to have taken her revenge by deliberately being late on the rare occasions when she *was* asked to appear. Hearing that he was furious at her late arrival on one occasion she said: 'Let him wait; it will do him good.' But always in the background was Alice Keppel whose hold on Alix's husband was so strong that nothing she could say would change a thing. Alix might well have said, as Diana Spencer was later to say, 'There were three of us in this marriage so it was a bit crowded.'

As King, Bertie insisted he needed an income from the civil list of £500,000 a year. He also knew he would never get it if he asked Parliament to pay his enormous debts, which amounted in 1901 to as much as £600,000. But Bertie was shrewd. Before discussing the matter with the Prime Minister he asked Ernest Cassel to set up a life insurance scheme that would pay off his debts within a few years. In fact, Cassel was so astute that the King's debts had been paid off by 1907. Parliament was so relieved not to have to pay the King's debts that they voted through the £500,000.

The money was supplemented by around £60,000 a year income from the Duchy of Cornwall estate, but even with these colossal sums Bertie still had to borrow occasionally from Cassel throughout his reign, and he would have sunk into far greater debt without Cassel's money-managing and investment skills – as well as the loans he made that were never to be repaid. Bertie also borrowed £100,000 from his old friend Rothschild and that too was never repaid.

Much of the money was used to run Sandringham, Balmoral and the King's other houses, but a great deal found its way to Mrs Keppel and the King's other women friends.

Bertie did well financially, even in comparison to his great-granddaughter HRH Queen Elizabeth, whose income increased 38 per cent between 2009 and 2014. Like Bertie, Elizabeth is astute – she insists on attending in person all meetings that discuss what she refers to as her 'salary'; she is shrewd enough to realise that the fact of her being at the meetings makes it very difficult for ministers and officials to argue with her or to refuse to give her what she wants. This personal involvement in these financial matters began with her great-grandfather.

Bertie became very ill indeed in 1902. He had been almost continually ill since his mother's death the previous year, but this was far more serious. Just days before his coronation was due on 26 June he had to have an operation to drain a large and very painful abdominal cyst. His doctors told him that he would die if they did not intervene. But in those pre-antibiotic days any operation carried the very real risk of death. Bertie's stomach had swollen massively in the weeks and months leading up to the operation and it was hard to know whether this was simply due to overeating or something far worse.

During the period before and after his operation, Alice Keppel was the only person Bertie wanted to see. She sat by his bedside holding his hand, but saying almost nothing. Queen Alexandra tried to comfort him when Alice was not there but her visits to his sickbed bored and irritated him. Alix complained that he pretended to be asleep when she visited him, and though this was true it was only partly because she bored the King; it had more to do with the fact that Bertie was trying to avoid exhausting conversations with a woman who was now so deaf that he had to bellow to be heard. Alix complained that she was just 'the woman in the cupboard' adjoining Bertie's suite of rooms – a feeling prompted by his obvious prefer- ence for Alice. With Alice constantly in attendance at the King's request, Alix had to swallow her pride and make herself scarce. She was forced to be polite to Alice when their paths crossed but pri- vately must have longed for the day when she could be rid of her.

Agnes Cook recalled that during all Bertie's illnesses and health scares, Alice became agitated and sometimes almost hysterical with worry. She went back and forth each day to Buckingham Palace, white with anxiety.

The whole atmosphere in the house at Portman Square changed when- ever Bertie's visits stopped and they only stopped when he was ill, but he was ill an awful lot after he became King. Mrs Keppel used to discuss the King's health with her husband – when the source of their money was at risk, worry brought them together. The servants didn't know exactly what they said to each other but the butler knew roughly what was going on. He told us that the Keppels discussed the fact that if the King died they knew they would have to change the way they lived. They might even have to retreat to Scotland or abroad.

The famous story of Queen Alexandra laughing when she saw, through the Sandringham windows, Alice in a carriage with Bertie – the two of them so fat they could barely squeeze in together – has the ring of truth about it. But Alix retained her formal loyalty to Bertie despite all his rebuffs and all her private reservations and unhappiness about his lifestyle.

Bertie's mother had been dead little more than a year, but in that time he had insisted on doing all the work she had formerly kept entirely to herself. He refused all offers of help and regularly sat up all night signing papers and trying to understand the vast piles of documents sent to him each day. But by now he was an old man and the work was difficult and exhausting.

In addition to the paperwork his mother had so jealously guarded, Bertie insisted on the importance of his public duties. He spent his days handing out medals and visiting the sick, opening hospitals and schools. He was obsessive about keeping control and keeping order. He also began to surround himself with pictures of his relatives just as his mother had done.

Even after his recovery from the operation to drain his abdominal cyst, when his health was better than it was ever to be again, his temper was rarely good and he shouted at his servants and advisors even when he was in the wrong. His equerries quailed before his rages. Alice Keppel calmed him and the equerries and other officials came to rely on her interventions on their behalf, but they resented the fact that they had to go through her and they particularly resented the fact that she so clearly enjoyed their need for her.

Even Alice occasionally fell foul of Bertie's temper. He had a particular hatred of bad card players and when Alice fluffed her hand during a game of bridge he was furious at being let down. He looked as if he was about to explode, but even as she apologised she made him laugh. She explained her failure by saying her difficulties had arisen because she 'could not tell the difference between a king and a knave'. It was a clever jibe that contained perhaps just a hint of how she must often have really felt about Bertie.

Bertie's coronation finally took place on 9 August 1902. He was determined to be a flamboyant, highly visible King, but he knew he would need Alice by his side to do it.

Westminster Abbey was filled with royalty and the aristocracy, but ever the rogue, Bertie made sure that a private gallery above the chancel was packed with his mistresses and former mistresses, including Alice Keppel, who insisted on sitting in the most prominent position. Among those in Bertie's 'loose box' were Agnes Keyser, the actress Sarah Bernhardt, Jennie Churchill and many others. Mistresses who were the wives of peers were allowed in the body of the church. As part of the coronation Bertie created more than 1,500 new knights and peers; many of these honours went to his friends and cronies and especially to those who had helped him financially. It was a form of corruption still with us today. Wealthy individuals donate large sums of money to one or other of the main political parties in return for honours. In 1902 the government *and* the King sold honours.

Agnes Cook recalled the frenzied atmosphere at the Keppels' home:

> Portman Square was crackling with excitement in the days leading up to the coronation. You might think that Mrs Keppel was about to be crowned Queen herself there was so much fuss, so much toing and froing, and of course in a sense she was being crowned Queen because poor Princess Alexandra was never really part of it. Mrs Keppel made it her role in life, both before Bertie's coronation and afterwards, to be available; she was at his beck and call night and day.

Alice Keppel's focus was always entirely on the King, but others noted Bertie's desperate need for *her*. The courtier Lord Esher commented that Bertie's admiration for Mrs Keppel was 'almost pathetic'.

At Portman Square, Agnes Cook remembered that the running and arrangement of the house was designed entirely with Bertie in mind and especially so now that he was King:

> My mother and the other servants were astonished that the refurbishment of the house included a private bathroom for Mrs Keppel and

another for her husband. All the servants were amazed by this – even the butler Rolfe and the cook Mrs Wright. In those days, baths were seen as slightly scandalous if you can believe it – they were seen as vaguely sexual and anyone who had a lot of baths (or more than one bath a week) was seen as up to no good. We knew that Mrs Keppel wanted to smell and look nice for the King. Being nice to the King was her job. It was what she got paid for and neither she nor Mr Keppel had any intention of doing anything that might make the King less likely to keep them on.

Alice was summoned regularly to Buckingham Palace while Bertie was recovering from his various ailments and bouts of general ill health, and the intensity and frequency of his visits to her after the coronation and when he was better increased.

Agnes Cook again:

He came at least once or twice a week except when he was at Sandringham, abroad or elsewhere. But when he was away she very often went with him, which is why poor Queen Alexandra stayed at home and became more reclusive. She felt the humiliation when the crowds shouted for Alice not for her. She was popular but she felt Alice was more popular. Even Bertie discussed domestic arrangements at Buckingham Palace, not with Alix, but with Alice.

When the King visited the house it was as if God had arrived – people kowtowed to royalty much more in those days. My mother was amazed when she occasionally heard that newspapers published criticisms of the King – she assumed the editors would be carted off to the Tower.

So a hush came over Portman Square when the King arrived and no one was supposed to be in the hall or on the stairs as he came and then an hour or two later as he left. It was stricter than it had been when he was just Prince of Wales. My mother said it was all ridiculous. And what was really funny was that if Alice made great efforts in her new bathroom for him, he certainly made no similar efforts for her. He was always rather smelly. You could smell it in the hall for hours after he left.

Only once did the gossips in the house get a glimpse of how Alice thought of Bertie the man rather than Bertie the King. My mother was sent up to clear the room where Alice had just been entertaining Bertie and she heard retching in the newly installed bathroom, and when Mrs Keppel emerged she was white and looked in pain.

As King, Bertie's insistence on working long hours on government papers was a foolish overreaction to the criticisms he knew were levelled at him privately that he was lazy and interested only in pleasure.

His reponse was to do far too much. It was as if he could do nothing if he did not do it to excess. Then, when he could do no more, he would set off to see Mrs Keppel or, less often, Agnes Keyser.

Bertie is usually credited with creating the *entente cordiale* between France and Britain. His real love for the wider European world stemmed more from the fact that he felt deeply European himself. Bertie the rake was never censored in France and Germany as he was in Britain. He could do as he pleased and, even with Alice on one arm, he could be sure the press would leave him alone. He loved it. In England it was all far more puritanical and censorious.

On a visit to France in 1903 the new King made speeches saying the British and French were old friends; he reviewed the troops, dined out every night, visited the theatres and generally made himself agreeable – in flawless French. The French newspapers decided they liked him and his visit became a huge success. He had always liked Paris and the French could tell that, in a sense, he was one of them. This certainly smoothed the path to good diplomatic relations between Britain and France, but it was the diplomats who really did the work. Bertie had some influence on the 1904 treaty between England and France that tried to settle various squabbles over colonial territories, but this again had more to do with creating a cordial atmosphere than negotiating the detail of any agreement. And further afield in Europe his influence was negligible. He could do nothing to reduce the hostility of his German relations, for example, and, as a result, within just four years of his death, Europe was to be plunged into one of the greatest military disasters in history.

Meanwhile, as Bertie and Alice's relationship became ever more platonic, the servants at Portman Square noticed Alice had picked up where she had left off – old lovers and new began to arrive once more for tea.

Agnes Cook noticed these changes:

Well, Bertie came as regularly as ever as the years went by, but one or two other men started to come to the house too, but only occasionally. They would disappear into Mrs Keppel's rooms and stay for an hour or so. One of them was a very wealthy banker; the other a friend of George's. The banker was an unattractive little man who virtually threw his hat and gloves at any poor devil who helped him off with his coat. We knew that Mrs Keppel was having sex with these men. She chose them carefully though and, after one or other had visited, there would always be the usual presents – flowers and crates of champagne. On one occasion a new carriage was delivered, much to the disgust of the coachman, who wanted one of the new-fangled motor cars!

But the main thing for Mrs Keppel was definitely sex because she never went to the theatre with her new lovers or anywhere else for that matter. It was too risky because, though the King had stopped having sex with her, he would have hated it if he thought she was having sex with other men while he just held her hand! So the visits of the other lovers were always very discreet and she made sure she was never seen in public with any of these men.

My mother used to explain how she and the other maids would make sure, if they could, that they went past Mrs Keppel's rooms a few times during her men friends' visits – domestic service is very, very boring you see and anything to alleviate the boredom was always welcome. The servants desperately wanted to know what Mrs K got up to and my mother used to say the grunts and groans coming from Mrs Keppel's rooms during these visits were disgraceful. It's odd isn't it how the servants in those days were far more puritanical and judge-mental about these things than the aristocrats they worked for?

But everyone could tell by the clothes and the jewels and pictures that arrived at the house that she was doing something.

With Bertie the grunts and groans had given way quite early in his reign to muffled laughter – I don't think they had sex much at all after about 1903 because he was enormous by then and had to stop walking every few seconds just to catch his breath. He must have been impotent by then, anyway. Who wouldn't be after the way he'd driven himself in terms of food, drink and prostitutes over the years? No one who lived as he lived could keep it up into his sixties.

While Alice Keppel was having sex with her new lovers, George Keppel continued with his old life. Agnes Cook again:

Mr Keppel looked after himself far more than the King ever did – he was careful about what he ate, loved the fact that he was still slim and dressed like a dandy. His routine was very strictly adhered to. He would spend the whole morning getting dressed with the help of his valet. He would then drive off to his club and perhaps go for a drive with one of his girlfriends afterwards. One night he brought two young ladies back after an evening at the theatre. This was a very rare event as he usually hated his rooms to be disturbed. After he'd slept with them or whatever he did with them, the servants were never really sure, there was a bit of a ruckus. The butler told my mother that when he arrived in George's rooms, George was red-faced and speechless in the middle of the room. He looked at Rolfe, the butler, and asked him to escort the young ladies to a cab. He then turned on his heel and locked himself in the bathroom until the girls had gone. Apparently, he never brought women back to the house again after that.

George adored his club too because it was so exclusive and he had only been able to get in after Bertie intervened. It was wall to wall earls, so he went there ever day just to sit there and show that he really was a member. It meant everything to him. But home was his retreat from the messy outside world and the one time he broke his rule he regretted it!

Like the English upper classes in general, George had no interest in his children until they had grown up. Bertie took a tougher line. Like his mother, he actively disliked his children. His son George, later King George V, said many years later that he had always been terrified of his father. All Bertie's sons feared him even if they did not actively hate him, but Bertie had a soft spot for little girls – especially if he suspected they were his.

To the astonishment of the servants at Portman Square, he even allowed Sonia Keppel to climb all over him during his visits – but then, as Agnes Cook says, she might well have been his daughter.

As the years passed and Bertie's health worsened, his need for Alice's company became almost desperate. In many ways his craving for Alice's company irritated the equerries and other royal hangers-on more than the couple's former sexual relationship. It was as if it was acceptable for a King to have sex with his mistress but unacceptable for him to like being with her or to seek her advice.

And as always there were those who not only resented Mrs Keppel's influence but who also actively disliked her. The notoriously ill-tempered Lady Lytton described Alice as 'coarse'. She hated the idea that Bertie had had a child with Alice and tried to scotch the widely believed rumours that Bertie was the father of Sonia. Lady Lytton described Sonia as looking 'far too Jewish' to be Bertie's offspring. But this was almost certainly Lady Lytton's haughty way of saying she knew that Mrs Keppel was sleeping with the King's Jewish banker Ernest Cassel or perhaps the Marquis de Soveral or both. If Mrs Keppel did sleep with Bertie's financial advisers in return for investment advice (which seems highly possible) it was probably not in the period 1898–1901 when Bertie would have been insistent that he alone had access to Alice's bed.

Despite the sniping, Alice still reigned supreme. Only very rarely was she left off an invitation – the Duchess of Portland refused to invite her to Welbeck, for example, feeling that Queen Alexandra would be upset, but the King was furious. Only rarely did Alice feel uncomfortable in her ambiguous role – it could be particularly awkward if she found herself in a country house to which the Queen had also been invited.

Almeric Fitzroy, who was clerk to the council, noted that at the card table at Wynyard Hall in County Durham, Alice seemed very conscious of the awkwardness of her position – she seemed a mixture of 'pride and humiliation', he noted. Despite her power and the King's insistence that she be allowed to go wherever he went, she had to go to embarrassing lengths to get round these problems. When the King visited Hatfield, for example, where the Marquess of Salisbury absolutely refused to invite Alice, she contrived to get an invitation to Lord Lytton's house just a few miles away at Knebworth to be near the King.

Such subterfuges would have caused her pain, but then she

inhabited a cruel and sometimes bullying world where, if you were unable to hold your own, you might easily sink without trace. And Alice was quite capable of causing others pain. At a party in London she was irritated by a pushy, over-talkative Jewish financier's wife. She suddenly snapped and said: 'My dear Maud, may I call you Lady Neumann?' No doubt it took poor Lady Neumann a moment or two to realise that she had been snubbed – it was a cruel jibe at her pride in her recent title.

In order to please the King and ensure his continued financial help, Alice put up with increasingly difficult social engagements. She also often had to sit up late with him since he was still absolutely insistent that no one was ever allowed to go to bed before him. It must have been horribly exhausting and boring, but Bertie always behaved like a petty tyrant and people deferred to him as if he had every right to be a tyrant. So long as Bertie continued to fund the Keppels' lavish lifestyle, Alice was prepared to put up with anything, but away from the court she often complained bitterly.

Agnes Cook recalled her mother's stories relating Alice's complaints about 'endless visits to country houses in winter where she was expected to hang around all day while the King shot thousands of pheasants'. Alice found it infinitely tedious and longed for the card table and trips to France where the King relaxed and was much better company. She also found the company of 'dull, stupid landowners from East Anglia and Shropshire' almost intolerable:

My mother said that Alice hated it when she had to visit the estates of English landowners. She thought they were stupid and provincial and she had a particular hatred for those with military pretensions. But she knew that English landowners could always be relied on to fawn and grovel before the King, which he of course loved. They also made sure he got the bulk of the birds on a shoot day. The host would mark the King's peg with a red flag so most of the birds could be directed over him.

It was all horribly obsequious.

More embarrassing still were the efforts of others to make sure that the King's mistresses could be accommodated without anyone knowing. William Le Poer Trench, who owned St Hubert's in Buckinghamshire, had his house removed from all local maps so that prying journalists and inquisitive locals would find it harder to locate the house and spy on the visitors.

Parliament was even brought in to protect the King's reputation when Le Poer Trench petitioned successfully to have a road diverted by an Act of Parliament so that passers-by would not get a glimpse of the King with Alice. More than twenty members of staff at St Hubert's were moved from their houses to accommodation further away to prevent any risk of embarrassment.

Meanwhile Alice grew ever richer. Bertie gave explicit instructions to Ernest Cassel that whenever Alice made losses on the markets, he should shoulder them. When she made gains, Cassel should pay all the money to her and take nothing back to compensate for her earlier losses. It was an extraordinary arrangement.

Cassel gave Alice's children expensive presents every year – including jewel-encrusted Fabergé eggs – and the children stayed regularly in his houses and flats in various parts of Europe. No wonder most people were convinced that Cassel was Alice's lover as well as her financial adviser. Of course the accumulation of capital was easier in 1900 than it is now; Cassel was a master of insider dealing, for example, and insider dealing was legal at that time.

Almost certainly at the instigation of the King, Cassel gave Sonia Keppel a very large cheque when she married in 1920.

Other businessmen and financiers who may well have slept with Alice, and who certainly helped her make her fortune, included Thomas Lipton of Lipton's tea fame and Sir Alfred Harmsworth, later lord Northcliffe, of the *Daily Mail*. To ingratiate themselves with the King in return for honours, these men and others like them helped Alice invest the money she received from her various lovers – so much so that when she died in 1947, Alice's fortune amounted to around £177,000, more than £10 million in today's values.

Intriguingly, some of her wealth was hidden away. In the 1980s a strongbox was opened after lying forgotten at Drummonds Bank at Trafalgar Square for more than forty years. It had been deposited on behalf of George Keppel. It contained a small mountain of fabulous jewellery – most given by the King to Alice – and included a massive diamond-covered nautical-themed brooch emblazoned with the words: 'Position quarterly and open. I am about to fire a Whitehead torpedo ahead.'

This was just the sort of sexual joke Bertie loved and, had it not been forgotten in that bank vault, then like almost every other scrap of evidence of Bertie's real character, it would no doubt have been destroyed. And it is easy to imagine why the Keppels might have confined such an item to a strongbox in a private bank.

Agnes Cook's mother recalled other vaguely pornographic gifts made by Bertie to Alice: 'She always had them put well away, my mother said, and she brought them out only when Bertie was about to pay a visit to her. He liked to see the diamonds, dresses and ornaments he had given her.'

※━━※━━※

As Bertie's desire for absolute control over his official duties as King took its toll, his occasional bouts of irritation and boredom became far more frequent. If one of his pens was in the wrong place on his desk or if his valet had forgotten to put out the exact number of cigarettes and cigars in his case each day, he would explode with fury. If his driver took a wrong turn he would bawl and shout until he was so enraged, he could hardly speak. He didn't care who he snapped at or humiliated; it was as if a spoilt child had, by some terrible mischance, been given the power to indulge his tantrums at will.

He could travel whenever he wished now and without consulting his 'eternal mother', but there was a desperate air to his constant desire for a change of scene. And somehow Alice always contrived to be nearby. Whenever he stayed with Cassel in the south of France it was a convenient cover for staying with Alice, who made sure she was also invited to the Villa Bellefontaine at the same time. But not everyone was happy with these arrangements – Cassel's daughter

Maudie complained, for example, that Bertie and Alice treated the Cassels as if they too were servants.

It is very difficult now to get an idea of the detail of Alice and Bertie's relationship during the long hours each week when, hidden from public view, they sat together and talked and held hands in the beautiful Georgian rooms at 30 Portman Square, rooms long ago demolished to make way for offices.

Agnes Cook gives us a unique glimpse of these private intimate moments; moments the couple enjoyed long after their sexual passion had ended:

I once saw them on the stairs together at Portman Square when they thought no one was watching. I had only recently started working for the Keppels – it would have been around 1908 when I was fourteen or fifteen. I had stopped in my tracks in the hall half-hidden when I heard Mrs Keppel's door to her private apartments open. I was terrified they might see me. They came down the stairs and stood looking at each other. The King was like a big barrel and she had put weight on too by this time. She stood and held his hand and looked straight in his eyes and smiled at him. He looked straight at her and smiled back and they just stood like that for what seemed a very long time before anyone moved. He had a puppydog look of adoration. Then he left and she carried on standing completely still, not looking after him but sort of staring into space. Her smile had gone and she almost had a look of exhaustion, as if the effort of being with him, with all his moods and grumpiness, was starting to be too much for her. She looked sad and worn out. It was the only time I felt sorry for her.

Mind you, I was very lucky they hadn't seen me or I might have been sacked for peeking!

But by 1907 Bertie was physically exhausted. Even the servants at Portman Square noted his decline, as Agnes recalls:

There was a shift, definitely. All the servants noticed it. As Prince of Wales he would walk up the stairs to Mrs Keppel's rooms with a sort of spring in his step. By 1907 his progress was slow and wheezy and he would stop a couple of times to catch his breath, and on one occasion there was a terrific incident.

The King had been with Alice one afternoon for an hour or so when there was a cry from the room. Rolfe the butler was always the nearest because, despite the rules that Knollys and Marlborough House tried to impose, the house at Portman Square had its own rules. Alice always wanted one of the maids and Rolfe on hand just in case something happened, because by around 1908 Bertie was ill – really ill. He was seriously overweight and his lungs barely worked. He had a cough that never went away – and on this particular day Rolfe heard the cry and a sort of thump and then knocked discreetly on the door.

Looking very flustered and red in the face, Alice shouted, 'Quickly!' and asked Rolfe to help lift the King back on to the sofa. He had slipped and fallen and been winded. What on earth he had been up to was hard to tell. But the family story was that he was trying to do something of which he was no longer capable. Rolfe rang for a maid to help clear up as a table had also been overturned and that was when I saw the mess. I curtsied to the King but he was so red in the face and wheezing so badly that I think a Hansom cab could have been driven into the room and he wouldn't have noticed. He just sat there with Alice at a discreet distance while Rolfe and I tidied up and then left the room.

But still the endless round of country house visits continued as well as Cowes in summer and visits to France and endless shooting weekends in winter, with all their awkwardnesses. And there were lavish lunches and dinners and official functions.

The Austro-Hungarian ambassador Count Albert Mensdorff recalled some of the difficulties that might arise when he described his enormous relief on hearing that Alice was not to attend a function at which he would have been obliged to present her. If he had refused she would make a fuss to the King who would then be angry with Mensdorff. But at the same time if he did present Alice then Queen Alexandra, who also planned to be at the function, would be upset. The idea that the Queen grew to accept and value Alice seems to have arisen as a result of early accounts of the relationship between Bertie and Alice that tried to gloss over its sexual aspects in favour of portraying Alice almost as a semi-official royal adviser. It was no doubt hoped that the shift of emphasis would be less damaging to Bertie's reputation. Others began to view Alice with less sympathy, too, but even on the political front she still had her admirers.

Bertie used her as a political tool when, for example, he insisted on her being placed next to one of his difficult relations at dinner so she could find out what was being thought and report back to him. She did this with the Kaiser, with whom Bertie was on bad terms, in 1907. With this in mind, Lord Hardinge of Penshurst famously paid tribute to Alice in his memoirs: he praised her discretion and loyalty to the King and said 'there were one or two occasions when the King was in disagreement with the Foreign Office and I was able through her to advise the King with a view to the policy of the government being accepted'.

This says something about Alice's diplomatic skills, but far more about how difficult ministers found it to deal directly with the increasingly bad-tempered King. And of course it is difficult to know whether Hardinge's praise was for public consumption only. Others said one thing about Alice publicly and something very different in private. She thought the Asquiths liked her, no doubt since they invited her to their dinner parties, and Herbert Asquith wrote to her at one point to praise her 'wise counsels', but to his own lover Beatrice Stanley he wrote that she was 'one of that pack of women for whom one cares least'.

This was typical of the reaction of politicians who knew Alice. They used her but resented the need to do it; they deplored the level of her influence with the King but recognised it was a fact with which they had to deal. Bertie refused to listen to reasoned arguments unless they came sugar-wrapped by Alice.

Despite the backbiting and gossip, Alice knew her value and simply brazened it out. But she was mocked in many quarters and especially when word got out that she had appointed what she described as her own lady-in-waiting, Lady Sarah Wilson.

Despite his impotence, Bertie's lifelong interest in young women continued; if he met someone and liked her, he would arrange to see her in private. His long-serving equerry Francis Knollys – 'the King's pimp' as Agnes's mother described him – would through discreet channels explain to the woman in question that Bertie had to be received in a certain way. The wonder of it is that so many women obeyed and did exactly as they were asked. Preparations were always as they were for the King's visits to Alice at Portman Square and to his other London mistresses. The protocol was precise.

During a visit to Germany in 1907 Bertie asked if he might call on 35-year-old Mrs Sophie Hall Walker, a champion golfer, at her hotel in Marienbad. Mrs Hall Walker was the wife of an immensely wealthy racehorse trainer. Bertie fell for her, probably because she had energy and drive and the sort of masculine personality he loved – she was also still slim and highly athletic.

The preparations for Bertie's afternoon visit were witnessed by 22-year-old Elsie Gill who told the story towards the end of her life to the writer Anita Leslie. Since then the story has reappeared in numerous biographies of Bertie because it is a rare first-hand account of the King's womanising; an account that shines out from the vast emptiness of documentation caused by the destruction of all Bertie and Alice's papers.

Elsie describes how, on the day of the King's visit, the hotel maids filled Mrs Hall Walker's room with flowers, and sprayed it heavily with scent. The curtains were then discreetly drawn. The servants were given strict instructions to stay out of the way when the door was locked at the appointed hour. Bertie always tried to ensure no one saw him actually visit any of his numerous lady friends; again a protocol insisted on by Knollys. The elaborate preparations were designed to create what the King saw as a seductive atmosphere, but Mrs Hall Walker probably had to endure little more than a few embarrassing fumblings and some intense hand-holding.

Agnes Cook confirms the description of these preparations given by Elsie Gill:

Well, occasionally an official from the palace – probably one of Knollys' lieutenants – would visit the house at Portman Square to make sure the rules of discretion were not slacking. The curtains were drawn by Rolfe or one of the maids perhaps half an hour before the King was due to arrive and the King himself always sent flowers on ahead so the room would be full of blooms. And scent was sprinkled every-where so the smell was almost overpowering.

Mr and Mrs Keppel expected absolute discretion and loyalty from their servants during these visits, but Buckingham Palace liked to make doubly sure there were no slip-ups. Of course the more fuss that was made the more the servants became intrigued, and there was a lot of anger about Mrs Keppel and the King and her other lovers. The servants weren't stupid and they were aware of the hypocrisies of the whole thing. Don't forget that some of us read the newspapers and servants were sometimes, though not often, radicals who hated the unearned privileges of the upper classes. My mother had a sort of love–hate relationship with the Keppels. She used to say that the Keppels and the King prostituted themselves because they knew no better; they'd never done a day's work in their lives; they were brought up in an atmosphere of immorality; they were parasites. It was exactly the sort of stuff published in the radical papers of the day. But she had a soft spot for Mrs Keppel at the same time and admired the fact that she'd made a fortune by getting the best price she could for her assets – her charm and her body. She used to say, 'If I'd have been as clever and good-looking as her I'd have done the same thing.'

Having been constantly criticised as a child, Bertie would brook no criticism as an adult. Most of his equerries and advisers had been born into families that had served the royals for generations, so they would have known that, with an occasional rare exception, a King's commands must always be obeyed, even if they were immoral or illegal – and Bertie's arrogance and impatience, his sense of absolute entitlement, were often reflected by the sense of entitlement deeply embodied in his well-born advisers.

The King very rarely apologised for outbursts of bad temper and always expected everyone to dance to his tune, but almost all his power in this respect related to his personal life. When he did as he pleased in the wider political world he often found himself in hot water. On one occasion he was forced to apologise to Prime Minister Asquith after deciding, on a whim and with no prior consultation, to appoint the Tsar of Russia Admiral of the British Fleet. And poor Bertie made himself look very foolish indeed when he announced that former Prime Minister Campbell-Bannerman had not done enough to deserve his peerage. The irony of this pronouncement would not have escaped Bertie's critics. The King was loaded with titles – at his birth he had been made Duke of Rothesay – and what had *he* ever done to deserve them?

As late as 1908 Bertie's youthful indiscretions were still occasionally catching up with him. He was forced, for example, to try to head off a public relations disaster involving his increasingly eccentric former mistress Daisy Brooke. He had not seen much of her in recent years because he felt she had become increasingly eccentric, if not mad – for Bertie, Daisy's madness was confirmed when she announced that she had become a socialist.

He was horrified when he heard she now made speeches to the workers regularly on street corners. Her aristocratic friends mocked her for shaking hands with members of the proletariat, but more serious efforts to curb her activities were brought to bear when it was discovered that she had discussed writing her memoirs and had even offered to sell her letters from Bertie to the *Daily Express*.

How she was prevented from doing so is now difficult to ascertain, but it seems that rather than threaten Daisy with legal action, Bertie simply wrote her a very large cheque, almost certainly on the advice of, among others, Alice Keppel.

And Bertie continued to be generous to other now discarded mistresses. He sent money to his old flame Emma Bourke, for example, after her husband lost all his money in 1907. The King arranged for the ever-willing Cassel to help her out. As long as they were discreet and made only mild threats, Bertie was usually willing to help his now ageing lovers or their husbands and children, but his motivation always was to ensure no further bad publicity. He had had his fingers burnt once too often to risk any stories about his affairs leaking to a press that could no longer be relied on to accept his view of things.

Alice Keppel was a key figure in this. She always encouraged him to settle amicably any difficulties with discarded women.

Agnes Cook recalled that:

Mrs Keppel often said that money might not always be the solution but it usually was. She persuaded the King to pay large sums and not just to a few well-known aristocratic former mistresses of the King. She also persuaded him to pay money to less well-born women he had slept with just once or twice and who had fallen on hard times. In his youth he had also paid for a number of abortions – the women he made pregnant were sent abroad. Sometimes they had their babies there, sometimes not.

Alice had sensed that the world was changing and the need for discretion was more important than ever. Indeed, a great deal of the written evidence about Alice at this time reveals that, as she grew older, she became almost almost paranoid about her privacy. Even Francis Knollys came under suspicion after she hinted that he might not be entirely reliable – Alice Keppel confirms this in a letter to Lord Rosebery. But her suspicions seem to have been far more about her own paranoia than about any real threat Knollys might have posed.

But if Alice sensed the world was changing, so too did the King and he did not like it. He and Alice were opposed to women being given the vote and he deplored the efforts of the suffragettes to achieve this. He was unashamedly reactionary – he hated the idea of women shooting, for example, and made huge efforts to stop women riding in Hyde Park unless they agreed always to ride side-saddle. He loathed the idea of women working in any capacity other than as wives, daughters and mistresses, as Agnes Cook recalled:

Oh he was a very crusty, old-fashioned sort of man. He thought women were meant to be decorative and charming – he thought of them as creatures designed to please men. He wouldn't have been able to think of them in any other way – except perhaps as bossy and interfering like his mother. I expect he didn't think of working-class women as women at all unless they were prostitutes. They were invisible drudges.

Servants like us knew very well the King's views on various topics because occasionally we would overhear something. Bertie's visits to Portman Square were not always as discreet as people think – he did occasionally say something out loud when a servant was within earshot. One day he was furious after he discovered that one or two politicians were sympathetic to the idea of women getting the vote. He always used the word 'socialist' to attack people who held new-fangled views such as female emancipation. And he talked about socialism as if it was the greatest crime in the world. 'Common vulgar socialists' was the phrase he used several times and Mrs Keppel would agree with him but also try to calm him down, not always successfully.

But if Bertie was furious about votes for women he was incandescent with rage about the so-called People's Budget of 1909, which proposed introducing taxes on large unearned incomes to pay for old-age pensions for the less well off.

Bertie's sole concern was to maintain the status quo, which meant not taxing those who lived on their investments. He and Alice were baffled by the government's desire for change. They had grown up in a world where the majority worked to keep a tiny minority in idleness so they were hardly likely to embrace a new world that overturned the old certainties. The world that was changing had been one where there really was one law for the rich and another for everyone else.

On a personal level Bertie and Alice often behaved as if they were above the law. As we have seen, they both adored gambling despite the fact that it was illegal, and when Bertie bought a motor car he insisted that his chauffeur should ignore speed limits. He expected the police simply to clear the way for him. But when Chancellor of the Exchequer Lloyd George made a speech in the summer of 1909 describing dukes and other aristocrats as parasites, there was nothing Bertie could do except shout impotently at anyone who would listen.

Agnes Cook recalled one of these outbursts:

> Everyone remembered the butler coming down to the servants' hall and saying 'The King is raging and throwing things about and Mrs Keppel is having a terrible time trying to calm him down'. Apparently she would lean towards him and look directly into his eyes often leaving her hand gently on his knee or on his shoulder; her voice was low, very deep and she talked in such an easy unaffected way, changing the subject now and then with hardly a moment's hesitation that her manner as much as anything acted as a sort of sedative.

Meanwhile Bertie continued to visit his German and Russian relatives, but little could be done about increasing anti-German feeling in Britain. It was almost as if the accumulation of arms and aggressive posturing had taken on a momentum that individuals were powerless to stop. Central to these difficulties was the simple fact that the Kaiser was almost certainly insane – his hatred of what he saw as the rotten corrupted English court was out of all proportion to any reality.

The Kaiser was so paranoid and filled with hate he managed to convince himself that Queen Alexandra was trying to poison him when she offered him medicine that she herself took regularly for her digestion.

With Alice Keppel's help, Bertie was persuaded to support the idea of an international conference and other measures to avoid confrontation, but tensions continued to mount. The King and the Kaiser might have been relatives but, if anything, this seemed to make matters worse. The spiral into a war that Bertie wouldn't live to see had begun.

Chapter 11

Goodbye, Bertie

B Y THE SPRING of 1909 Alice was increasingly concerned about the King's health. She had spoken gently to him about taking more care of himself in general but she knew better than to try to force him to change. It would have destroyed the basis on which their relationship had always thrived – she was the infinitely indulgent mother he had never had and change at this late stage, even if it meant prolonging the King's life, was simply not possible. Alice and his doctors suggested he merely reduce his smoking and eating. His refusal was absolute. He made it clear that he would rather die than not smoke or gorge himself at the table.

It was around this time that the strain of coping with a King who might die at any time began to show in Alice.

Agnes Cook recalled her 'constantly worried air'. She also became

> forgetful and uncharacteristically short-tempered. She looked pale and distracted and we thought it was probably that she was wondering how she would cope if and when the King died. He had been central to her life for so long she probably panicked when she thought of life without him. In the Keppel household the King was far more important than George – even George knew it.

Despite the widespread feeling that nothing could be done to change Bertie's lifestyle, many of his advisers were privately disgusted by his eating habits which seemed to have grown worse as his health declined. Elsie Wright, who worked for some time at Sandringham, recalled that at meals, whether alone or in company, the King 'never chewed his food but gulped it down whole as if it might at any time be snatched away from him. The noise of his eating could sometimes be heard in the corridor.'

At Sandringham towards the end of 1908 Bertie was so ill he took to his bed for ten weeks. This was followed by a trip to Brighton where Alice was waiting to comfort him.

At this distance in time and with the almost total destruction of Alice and Bertie's correspondence it is very difficult to capture the flavour of the endless conversations the two must have enjoyed when they were out of the spotlight. But one window on this history does exist. Agnes Cook kept an unpublished account written by her mother of several admittedly short conversations overheard between Alice and Bertie.

Like almost all servants at the time, my mother was so dazzled by being in the same house – and occasionally in the same room – as royalty that she wanted to write down an account of what she had seen and heard.

She describes hearing Alice praise one of Bertie's closest friends in a teasing way that made the King laugh loudly. He would tilt his head back and almost chuckle before saying, 'I know, he is wonderfully absurd.' Alice would continue with her gossipy jokes about their mutual acquaintance but never saying unkind things about whoever they were discussing – she just exaggerated their oddities or idiosyncrasies. Her talk brought various individuals to life in a sort of highlighted way – she was very good at flights of comic fantasy where one thought led to another.

She once said of Francis Knollys, 'Yes, he is marvellous but his moustache is perhaps the most marvellous thing about him.' That was typical of her teasing – harmless but with perhaps a tiny bit of hidden malice that you only really noticed later. Bertie could never get enough of it.

But at least by now Bertie was past being sexually demanding, and for Alice and the other women he still visited this must have been a great relief, since any exertion might easily have killed him and a dead King at Portman Square would be difficult to explain.

Agnes again:

> By 1909 he really looked permanently very unwell. But he liked just being with Alice and continuing with a visiting routine that had become part of his life. The most he got up to was simply pressing his hand against her bosom. It was as if he had only his memory of passion and was astonished to find it had gone. An occasional caress was perhaps just a slightly baffled attempt to re-ignite a fire long extinguished.

Through the winter of 1909–1910 Bertie continued his round of country house visits to friends who were increasingly accused by the radical newspapers of being rich layabouts. He stayed at the Duke of Westminster's estate in Cheshire and then at Elveden, the famous East Anglian pheasant-shooting estate, and then moved to Sandringham for New Year's Eve. Alice Keppel was always there but usually in the background during the day and then by the King's side at dinner. Alix was, as so often, nowhere to be seen. Alice was the perfect wife Bertie had never had and in Brighton in the New Year of 1910 she could be seen regularly walking arm in arm with the King, who no longer cared who saw them together. The newspapers reported that the couple seemed blissfully happy, though they were obliged to stop now and then so that Bertie could catch his breath. Mrs Keppel was, on the other hand, distinguished by her vigour, though by now she was rather stout.

But the signs that something was seriously amiss would have been clear by the mid-summer of 1910. Bertie apparently looked dreadful. Alice must have known that the King to whom she had devoted the past twelve years of her life had not long to live.

Bertie set off in March 1910 for Paris where he met several former mistresses, including the Comtesse de Pourtalès, but his days of visiting Parisian brothels were over. From Paris he set off for Biarritz, which had always been his favourite European resort, and the ever-faithful Alice accompanied him. According to Agnes Cook, the gossip in the house before Alice left for France was that she was alternatively terrified and distraught that Bertie would soon be gone for ever.

'She was so upset, my mother recalled, that despite her extraordinary powers of self-control, she was often seen red-eyed or in tears.' It would have been clear to her that Bertie was now very ill indeed.

Her panic was understandable. With Bertie gone she would almost certainly be banished from court; her place in society generally would also be compromised because she was now so clearly linked in the minds of the public with Bertie that she could never pretend they had simply been friends who moved in the same circles. Her husband George was rarely mocked for his complaisance, but as soon as the King died he too would lose his special status, and of course both Alice and George would lose the vast financial advantages Alice's years in the royal bed had guaranteed. The couple were on the brink of a change so vast that they must have been terrified even to contemplate it.

Without the King, Alice would have to forge a new place in

society and that would not be easy. George might easily become the butt of cruel jokes that had long been kept at bay by the prospect of the King's power and potential displeasure. As it turned out Alice and George's lives were to be changed far more than even they suspected; the King's death was to usher in a more democratic, less deferential world where taxes, a new puritanical King and changing social attitudes forced the Keppels, ultimately, into almost permanent exile in Italy.

But all this was still some time in the future when Alice saw Bertie collapse with a serious bout of bronchitis soon after arriving in Biarritz. His cough was accompanied by what his doctors diagnosed as a distinct weakening of his heart. His English nurse, who was rushed out to him, thought there was a very real danger of pneumonia from which the already weak King would almost certainly not recover.

In her book *Ask Sir James: The Life of Sir James Reid, Personal Physician to Queen Victoria*, Michaela Reid records that Sir James thought Alice Keppel was convinced the King would not survive. She appeared to be on the verge of hysteria. Reid, who had earlier diagnosed the King with gonorrhoea, knew that though the King might recover this time, his weakened, diseased heart meant he could not live long whatever his doctors did. Despite concealing this from the family it is unlikely he was able to conceal the truth from Alice Keppel.

The British newspapers reported that the King was only mildly indisposed and the general panic about his health was overtaken by the constitutional crisis which was to lead, ultimately, to a severe curtailment of the House of Lords's powers. Having rejected the so-called People's Budget, the lords were told that Asquith would ask the King to create a sufficient number of peers to ensure the budget was voted through. Bertie hated the idea as he felt the poor should not be made better off at the expense of the rich landowning class. Politicians and newspaper editors complained that attempts by the King – and the House of Lords – to stop the democratically elected House of Commons passing its budget could lead to the end of the monarchy.

Bertie's illness was no doubt made worse by these political changes to which he so violently objected. But he knew he was trapped and that the world he loved was coming to an end; the new world with its ghastly hints of socialism was a world he did not wish to live to see.

Against all the odds, Bertie seemed to rally and by the end of March 1910 he was dining out every night and eating his usual enormous quantities of rich food. He was also smoking as much, if not more than ever. Perhaps fearing the worst he kept Alice continually by his side, but also summoned his former mistresses Agnes Keyser and Jennie Churchill to Biarritz.

Often bored and with no real occupation, Bertie no doubt appreciated Oscar Wilde's joke from *The Importance of Being Earnest* that smoking at least gave a man an occupation. He had struggled his whole life to overcome the idea deeply drilled into him as a child that he was useless and unfit to be the son of his parents.

By the end of April 1910 he appeared to some to be saying goodbye to the world. He seems to have had an inkling that he did not have long. As he left Biarritz he murmured that he was saying goodbye to Biarritz perhaps for good, and back in London when Lord Redesdale saw him at the opera, he reported that the King, alone in his box, sighed and looked sad.

Between Friday, 29 April 1910 and the following Monday the King's health took a sudden and very dangerous turn. He seemed calm, although quiet, on the Saturday but insisted on working on his government papers throughout Sunday. On Monday he visited his former mistress Agnes Keyser, who immediately sent a note to his doctor saying how unwell he seemed. By midnight on Monday he could hardly breathe and had to be given morphine. Next day he seemed better, but there was one extremely worrying development – throughout that long day he ate nothing.

Playing cards with Alice Keppel that evening and despite terrible difficulties breathing, he carefully prepared and lit a large cigar which he seemed to enjoy immensely. Smoking, which killed him in the long run, comforted him in the hours before his death.

By the time Alice returned home to Portman Square late that night she was in a terrible state, as Agnes Cook recalled:

> That was the worst period of all. Mrs Keppel locked herself in her room, had frantic discussions with George, returned to her room, sent for George – it was awful. She and George had hardly spoken for years but now they were often together trying to decide what on earth they would do if the King died – by now of course it was more when the King died. I saw Mrs Keppel on the stairs looking completely discomposed; her hair was untidy, she was pale and at one point she seemed to be biting her nails. This was amazing for the staff

because Mrs Keppel had always been completely in control and perfectly dressed and manicured – no one had ever seen this side of her and it was almost frightening.

By Wednesday large black blotches had appeared on the King's skin and he was subject to violent coughing fits. He must have known he was dying because he said on being told he should go to bed, 'No, I shall work to the end.'

Alice seemed to be the only person who could comfort him when, on Thursday of that week, he had to be given oxygen repeatedly. Gone were her jewels and fine dresses. She arrived in a plain day dress and coat, looking ill and worried. Despite being now seriously ill, Bertie insisted on trying to work. It was, at some deep level, his way of proving that he was not after all as lazy as his mother had always believed. He worked on, despite the fact that his heart was on the verge of collapse – the evidence was clear in the permanent blue tint in his complexion. His heart was beginning to fail to supply enough oxygen to keep his body going.

His breathing growing ever worse, still he refused to go to bed, and Alice refused to leave him. He sat up the whole night in a chair and then, only hours from death, insisted on standing up despite being barely conscious. It was a bizarre echo of the final hours of his ancestor Elizabeth I, who stood motionless for a full sixteen hours before she died.

Money had always been at the heart of Bertie's life and even now, as he prepared to depart from it, money complicated the issue. His old friend Sir Ernest Cassel was summoned and he left a wad of

£10,000 in cash by the side of the dying King, as if more money might save the life of a man who had spent untold millions on luxuries throughout his life. Rumour then and now suggested he had asked Cassel to bring the money so he could give it to Alice – a parting gift that he must have known would be the last from the royal coffers.

As Bertie lost control of his body so he lost control of those around him. For years he had been able to summon Alice and his other mistresses whenever he liked, but as he slipped into unconsciousness, Alice was banished from the palace by Queen Alexandra.

Knowing that this was what would probably happen if he slipped into a coma, Bertie had given Alice a letter sometime previously. It is an extraordinary document and it gave Alice a final taste of the power she had enjoyed for more than a decade but was soon finally to lose for ever. It read:

MY DEAR MRS GEORGE

Should I be taken very seriously ill I hope you will come and cheer me up, but should there be no chance of my recovery, you will I hope still come and see me – so that I may say farewell and thank you for all your kindness and friendship since it has been my good fortune to know you. I feel convinced that all those who have any affection for me will carry out the wishes I have expressed in these lines.

When Alice was told in these final hours that she was not welcome at the palace, she immediately ensured this letter reached the hands of Queen Alexandra.

Bertie hated the idea that Alice would not be near him when he died – hence the last line of the letter which is clearly his way of demanding that Alexandra should do something he knew she would not want to do.

Alix was not prepared to ignore the letter and so she had no choice but to allow Alice to visit her lover on his last day on earth. If the letter was also Bertie's way of trying to ensure Alice would not be banished from court after his death, it failed. It was just as it had been when the dying Charles II implored those around him: 'let not poor Nellie starve'. He'd hoped that Nell Gwynn would not be spurned by the court after he died. Like Bertie, Charles was leaving a dying instruction that his mistress should be treated well after his death. Nellie was given a grant for life. Alice was not so lucky.

It is extraordinary that Alice entertained hopes that the Queen she had supplanted for more than a decade would do anything other than take her revenge once Bertie was dead. Alice's sense of her own importance and appeal no doubt clouded her judgement; she was the King's mistress – virtually, she believed, his wife – and she felt that this should ensure she was treated well by Queen Alexandra and the other members of the royal family. But it was precisely her closeness to Bertie that ensured she would be shut out. Throughout history royal favourites have, ultimately, been destroyed: from Edward II's Piers Gaveston to the late Queen Mother's servant William Tallon, or 'Backstairs Billy' as he was known. With royal patronage gone, the court always turns on outsiders.

Alice arrived early in the evening of the King's last day, 6 May, and according to Bertie's courtier Viscount Esher, who later wrote a book about Edward VII, Alice was so distraught that she had to be bundled out of the King's room after he lost consciousness. Esher insists the Queen was polite to Alice, but even if Esher is a reliable source, which is by no means certain, there is no doubt that Alice felt the icy chill felt by all royal mistresses when they face final banishment.

After a series of heart attacks throughout that day, the King died late in the evening. No sooner had he died than a power vacuum developed at Buckingham Palace. No one really knew what to do, but Queen Alexandra was able at last to monopolise her husband in death in a way she had never been able to do in life. Forced to allow Alice to be with the King while he was still conscious, she changed the instant he slipped into his final coma. In a blunt aside to Bertie's doctor that would have been audible to Alice, she said, 'Get that woman out of here.'

By all accounts Alix was deeply upset by his death, but the idea that she had never ceased to love Bertie, despite his treatment of her, is probably rather fanciful. Conspiracy theories also filled the vacuum, with various people claiming that the row over forcing the King to create hundreds of new peers had caused his death; others claimed the King had died of cancer of the throat caused by syphilis. He may well have had syphilis or cancer or both, but the immediate and obvious cause of his death was heart failure caused by obesity and heavy, continuous smoking.

Distraught and out of control, Mrs Keppel seems to have made uncharacteristically wild statements following the King's death. In his biography of Lord Rosebery, Leo McKinstry says Alice confided to Rosebery that the King had repeatedly complained to her that his Queen was cold and undemonstrative, and by that she meant not only emotional coldness but also sexual coldness. Of course the remark, even if true, might be seen as a variation of the old line by the married man who says to his mistress 'my wife doesn't understand me'.

Alice was so shocked by what had happened that she refused to return to the house in Portman Square. Instead, she stayed with a friend in nearby Grafton Street and, legend has it, wept for days. But the King's gifts of money, jewellery, furniture and antiques meant that, though Alice would now have to start a new life away from the centre of things, it would still be a life cushioned by a decade and more of having her 'fists in the money bags', as Virginia Woolf put it.

She might've been financially secure, but socially she was suddenly very insecure indeed. Courtiers and members of the royal family, who had greeted her warmly when the King was alive, began to turn on her.

It is extraordinary, in fact, that with her shrewd knowledge of political and social affairs at the highest level, she did not see more clearly quite how completely she would be shunned once her royal protector had died. Her sense of her own indispensability had blinded her to the reality of life as a royal mistress. Suddenly she had few, if any, friends at court and among the aristocracy more generally it was only her old friends and lovers who stood by her.

In the coming months, rather than wait for invitations that might never come, she went on the offensive. She organised her own lunches and dinner parties as if her life depended on it, which, in a way of course, it did.

Cynics said that the old Marlborough House set were, in the main, too frightened to snub Mrs Keppel's soirées because they were fully aware that she knew who had slept with whom, who cheated at cards, who was massively in debt, who had lied to whom, and so on. The best way to avoid malicious gossip was to remain part of the Keppels' inner circle, but it was a circle that no longer overlapped with royal circles.

A great change had come about and the wider world noted it. An article in *The Clarion*, never very sympathetic to the royals, recognised the new world and said good riddance to the old: 'Yes, it is truly the end of an era; an era in which a gross monarch behaved as if he was above the law and above the rules of decency. No doubt his concubines will now slowly melt away as the new and more serious age begins to dawn.'

The reality of the new order dawned on Alice when, sometime after the King's death, she set off for Marlborough House, scene of so many of her triumphs. Her aim was simply to sign her name in a book of condolences. She presumably had no intention of trying to speak to Bertie's son, soon to be King George V, nor any other member of the royal household, but instructions had been given that under no circumstances was Mrs Keppel to be allowed into the building.

The poet and horse-breeder Wilfrid Scawen Blunt reveals perhaps better than anyone how Queen Alexandra really felt about the

King's mistresses. According to Blunt, soon after the King died Alix confided to Sir Francis Laking how she had felt about the King's womanising: 'I was so angry about Lady Warwick and the King expostulated with me and said I should get him into the divorce court. I told him once and for all that he might have all the women he wished and I would not say a word.'

The hurt combined with resignation speaks volumes. But now that Bertie was dead there need be no fear of the divorce courts. Queen Alexandra could at last assert herself and no longer put up with the endless humiliations of the King's mistresses – 'the whores and strumpets of a corrupt court', as *The Clarion* newspaper put it.

For Alice, all contacts with the royal family and Buckingham Palace were severed, but worse was to come. Alice tried new approaches – she even contacted the Kaiser, the dead King's nephew, but he also refused to see her.

The £10,000 in cash that Ernest Cassel had hurriedly left with the King a short time before he died, and that was almost certainly intended as a parting gift to Alice, did not reach her. The money was returned to Cassel, who promptly sent it back with a note to say it was the King's money not his. No doubt it disappeared into the royal coffers. It certainly never reached Alice.

Despite her grief, Alice organised almost continuous luncheon parties. These gave her something to focus on, but she knew greater changes were necessary if she was to survive. She began to see that much of her old life and its associations would have to be jettisoned. She arranged to move from 30 Portman Square and the move took place that summer. Agnes Cook's mother recalled the chaos:

After the King died Mrs Keppel took to her bed – but not in the Portman Square house. She moved to a friend's house on the other side of the square. Some said it was to avoid the attentions of the newspaper journalists keen to ask her questions about the King, but it was also because the Portman Square house had really been the house she shared with the King. Without him she hated it. Her daughters were sent away too – she didn't want to see anyone for a while after the King died.

But old habits die hard and Alice's essential optimism began to reassert itself. She wrote to all those who might best be described as part of the inner circle and she did it almost before she had really come to terms with the King's death. In fact, in her haste she upset those who believed that any socialising during the period of official mourning for the King was bad form.

In a letter to Lady Knollys, which is typical perhaps of Alice's subtle equivocation, she suggests that no one could possibly think of entertaining in the midst of such grief but it is fine if entertaining consists in seeing just a few friends. Perhaps this was fair enough given that Alice was famous for inviting up to seventy people to one of her usual dinners. She wrote:

DEAR LADY KNOLLYS,
I feel sure that you cannot think I should give a dinner party, feeling as I do. Tomorrow Soveral, Louise Sassoon and Captain Fortescue

come. Soveral because he does not dine out and I told Lord Knollys of Louise who is coming up simply to see me. How people can do anything I do not know, as life with all its joys has come to a full stop at least for me.

Alice implies that, rather than organising dinner parties, she is simply organising gatherings at which old friends might discuss the late King. The distinction was lost on many and cynics argued that it was simply Alice Keppel's instinct for survival trying to ensure that she remained friends with as many as possible of those who had given her life meaning.

Having been told by the new King that she was not welcome to sign the book of condolences, Alice tried other means to ingratiate herself with the new regime. She offered to look after Caesar, the late King's elderly and very bad-tempered dog. This also was refused despite the fact that Queen Alexandra hated the dog. Worse was to come when George Keppel was not invited to the King's funeral. Alice had been invited, but that was unavoidable – it would have caused more fuss and more attention from the press if she had not been invited. If she was there, the fiction could be maintained that she had only ever been a friend of the late King. Not inviting her would suggest she had been something far more important than that.

To the disgust of some, Alice wore full widow's mourning to the funeral which was held at St George's Chapel, Windsor on 20 May. But once the funeral was over Queen Alexandra and her son, the new King George V, were determined that Bertie's sordid past and all those who were part of it should be consigned, as far as possible, to social oblivion. Wilfrid Scawen Blunt wrote that the new King hated the Jews and women with whom his father had spent so much time: 'He hates all these and will have nothing to do with them.'

Blunt also recorded a commonly held view of obituaries published by conservative and liberal newspapers after the King's death: 'The absurdities written about him in every newspaper pass belief ... according to strict theology he is most certainly at the present moment in hell.'

The queue to see the King's coffin, as he lay in state at Westminster Hall sometime earlier, had stretched for miles and the streets were thick with onlookers when his cortege made its way to Windsor. The King was more popular in death than he had been in life – his hedonism and love of women had endeared him to a large section of the populace fed up with the dull, worthy years of Queen Victoria. Bertie had come to be seen as a merry, almost Falstaffian figure in his final years.

As the weeks passed after the funeral, people became aware at some level that the world had subtly changed: compared to his father, George V was likely to be a dull, if worthy, monarch and one who loathed everything his father had most loved.

Meanwhile the heyday of the aristocracy was ending; taxes long mooted were soon to shift the financial balance of power. Pressure for Home Rule in Ireland was growing, women were soon to get the vote. A new world was coming and the old guard hated it.

Chapter 12

Beginning
Again

A S THE WEATHER warmed that year, Alice
and George were invited to Lord Curzon's
grand house in Hampshire. This was Alice's
first real step back into the wider world fol-
lowing the death of the King. But according to servant gossip she
had to force herself to go, as Agnes Cook explains: 'She was still
both upset at how her life had changed but also embarrassed at the

widespread discussion of how she had broken down in the King's bedroom on the last day of his life and screamed so hysterically that she had to be forcibly removed.'

George Curzon was one of the richest men in England and for Alice a visit to his house must have reminded her of past glories. There was no shooting as there had been on so many of her previous winter visits with Bertie, but there was tennis and croquet and in the evenings long, gossipy dinners and cards. Inevitably servants were everywhere and they noticed that despite her grief over the death of Bertie, Alice was already returning to her dominant flirtatious mode.

Agnes Cook again:

More than anything she loved intrigue and she loved to know who was sleeping with whom so that over dinner she could gently tease and gossip. It was so ingrained in her that even with the King only recently dead she always livened up over dinner. Several of the servants who went with her to Hackwood House (the Curzon's home) noticed that she was as bright and sparkling as ever.

I went along with Alice Keppel's lady's maid. I hadn't a clue why I had been asked because it was unusual to take more than a lady's maid, but it turned out that I was needed to maid for one of the other women guests, a young unmarried woman.

Anyway, I remember the Hackwood House staff laughing in the servants' hall and being told off by the butler for gossiping about people swapping bedrooms all through the night. Mrs Keppel supposedly left her room or so one of the footmen told me.

By November 1910 the Keppels had decided drastic action was required. The quiet lunches and country house visits to their remaining friends had lost their appeal and had not revived the couple's former glittering life. Alice decided that it would be good for the family to go on a world tour while the couple's new house at 16 Grosvenor Street was being altered and redecorated. The tour would include Ceylon (now Sri Lanka) and China and the family would be absent for at least two years. It was a natural solution to an otherwise intractable problem. Perhaps Buckingham Palace would learn to forgive and forget while they were away. Alice gave out that their grand tour was designed to complete their daughters' education but few believed her. Typical of her teasing was her comment that 'No young lady's education can be considered complete without a smattering of Tamil'.

If England now viewed Alice Keppel with a measure of disdain, the same was not true on the Continent. There she was still treated as if she really was royalty. Her wealth and former social position, not to mention her habitual grand manner, ensured that wherever she went she would be treated with the respect and deference now so sadly lacking in London.

The Keppels did not travel across the world alone. Alice's brother Archie, whom she had kept financially secure all these years, accompanied her with his son Ronnie and his son's family. Alice, as ever, paid the bills on the way out but reduced costs by staying in a friend's villa in Ceylon. The villa was owned by the Lipton family that had long employed George Keppel in a well-paid job that required very little work.

Perhaps because they were in trade – always a sign of lower caste in Edwardian England – the Liptons never failed to be impressed and awed by Alice and George.

While the Keppels and their friends spent their time hunting big game in Ceylon, Alice's two daughters Sonia and Violet were sent back to London and then on to Munich to learn German. The choice of German was no doubt a homage to Bertie, who had always felt that Germany was his real home.

The locals in Ceylon and China seemed to believe that Alice was actually a member of the British royal family, so grand was her entourage, which may explain why it was easy to fob the locals off when someone in the party ran over and killed an elderly woman. The English seem to have seen the accident as a mere inconvenience. It is recalled in a curiously cold and detached tone by Sonia Keppel in her book *Edwardian Daughter*, but then at the time she was writing, native peoples across the world were still viewed by the British as scarcely human. But it was Alice's sense of her own importance and the size of her obviously wealthy party that seems to have impressed people wherever she went.

Agnes Cook remembered this aspect of Mrs Keppel's character:

> I think being with the King so long and being treated by the public
> and the court as if she were the 'real' Queen made her adopt ways of
> behaving, speaking and even walking that she could never shake off.
> When she travelled she had a sort of grandeur that made everyone

kowtow to her. She had no official status, especially in foreign countries, yet she behaved as if deference were simply her due and people responded to that.

I think this sense of her own importance stayed with her for the rest of her life. Everyone knew that Queen Alexandra had tolerated Bertie's mistresses because she believed they were an amusement for Bertie that he couldn't do without, but that his real love was reserved for her. Alice would have disagreed with this. She was convinced that Bertie really loved her and not his wife and that therefore in the strange world she inhabited she was more Queen than the real Queen.

The Keppels all returned to London in the spring of 1912 and Alice began again to try to rebuild some kind of life, but life for her meant a busy social life meeting and dining with people at the highest level, gossiping and intriguing. Having enjoyed this for so long she must have hated the idea of long, lonely evenings stretching ahead endlessly, and she was determined to make sure society, or at least some part of it, welcomed her.

The London the Keppels returned to must have seemed a cold and sombre place, but at least they had escaped the grim awfulness of that first winter following the King's death. Alice was nothing if not resourceful, but even she must have known that she would not be able to pick up her old life quite where she had left it. She knew she had enemies – Lords Salisbury and Esher among others – so as soon as her new house was ready, she carefully cultivated those who were more sympathetic, whose attitudes and interests matched hers. She was also careful to set up a series of extravagant luncheons that people would find it very difficult not to attend.

'They were incredibly lavish,' remembered Agnes Cook,

and only the old die-hards in the circles close to Queen Alexandra refused to come, as well as the new generation at Buckingham Palace that surrounded the new King. They never came. I remember the Asquiths were often there and Mrs Keppel's old neighbour and lover from Portman Square, Lord Alington was still drooling over her.

Alice was also careful only to invite those who sympathised with her rather cynical view of marriage. In short, she cultivated those who remained loyal to adultery as a sport.

Agnes Cook again:

Mrs Keppel's friends, or at least those who came to the new house in Grosvenor Street after her two-year holiday, were mostly part of the wife-swapping set, I think. I hadn't worked for the Keppels for that long, but even I knew after a short time who slept with whom. It was always being talked about in the servants' hall.

During a 'Friday to Monday' – a weekend away – a servant would be told to put little labels on each bedroom door so that when the various couples changed rooms at night there were no embarrassing mistakes, although the people we worked for were so randy they often used to spice things up by deliberately making mistakes so they could get to sleep with someone else's mistress. No one ever seemed to complain whatever happened.

But we all had a shock when the Keppels got back from their tour abroad after the King died – Mrs Keppel's hair had gone completely white. At first we thought how terrible and we felt sorry for her because we thought it was the beginning of the loss of her looks, but actually I think she'd been dying her hair for years and she'd sort of given up as she was now middle-aged. That was the gossip from the lady's maid anyway.

As soon as she got back into her stride in England with country house visits pursued with a vengeance, I don't think she worried about her hair at all. She very quickly started sleeping with rich men again; it was in her blood; it made her life fun. She'd always done it and she loved it so it was hard to stop. She liked rich and powerful men who would give her wonderful gifts in return for sex – and who can blame her?

She used to think married women who didn't sleep around were letting their husbands down. I later read that she tried to explain this theory to Winston Churchill's wife Clementine, but Clementine was apparently horrified at the idea.

According to Agnes, Mrs Keppel once confessed to her lady's maid that if she could not see people, dine out, play cards and travel, she would die or go mad.

Sonia and Violet had stayed in Germany for more than a year after the Keppels returned to London from their Far East tour. The idea was to perfect their German – a language that was soon to become very unpopular indeed in England – but also to distance them from the changes that were taking place in their parents' lives.

Like all members of the governing classes at this time Alice and George had had little to do with their children while they were growing up. Alice only began to be interested in Sonia and Violet when the time approached for them to be introduced to society and married off.

Her desire for her children to live in absolute conformity with her own standards was to cause a huge rift with her daughter Violet, who was to rebel violently against what she saw as the lies and hypocrisy of her mother's life. Violet simply could not accept that one should marry for the sake of appearances and then sleep with dozens of different men for money as her mother had done. Their differences on this subject were to cause years of heartache for both women.

Violet developed a highly idealised view of relationships in response to her mother's life and she was famously to reject the standard upper-class English idea of marriage as a passport to adulthood and society when she began an affair with the writer Vita Sackville-West, an affair painfully described in a memoir written by Vita Sackville-West's son Nigel, long after both Violet and Vita were dead.

But as early as 1913 the signs of rebellion were there. Alice began to worry about Violet, thinking she was both highly impractical, volatile and unstable.

While Violet's future was being discussed, every effort was being made to turn 16 Grosvenor Street into a salon without equal in London. Agnes Cook remembers the frenzied atmosphere of the time:

> We were rushed off our feet from the end of 1912, I think, almost until the outbreak of war. Lunches were organised with military precision and the most luxurious foods were ordered. The dining room had an enormous table that seventy or more could sit round and it would take the footmen and maids hours to get it ready each day. The butler would measure the distance between plates and table decorations, between knives and forks to ensure everything was absolutely symmetrical.

Number 16 Grosvenor Street was an immensely grand eighteenth-century house that had declined a little in the nineteenth century – the ground floor had become a piano shop – but it was big enough for each member of the Keppel household to have a complete set of rooms of their own. According to Osbert Sitwell it was

> ...surely one of the most remarkable houses in London. Its high façade, dignified and unpretentious as only that of a London Georgian mansion can be, very effectively disguised its immense size. Within existed an unusual air of spaciousness and light, an atmosphere of luxury, for Mrs Keppel possessed an instinct for splendour, and not only were the rooms beautiful, with their grey walls, red lacquer cabinets, English eighteenth-century portraits ... huge porcelain pagodas

and thick magnificent carpets, but the hostess conducted the running of her house as a work of art in itself.

While preparations went on for a seemingly endless series of grand luncheons, George hid away in his apartment on the top floor. Here he could be undisturbed and lead his own life, as Agnes Cook recalled:

Well, George Keppel was a funny one. He had his own bathroom and sitting room and had to have it just so – he had more perfumes and potions than his wife! We used to call him 'Her ladyship'. His walls were covered with photographs of young women and his little tables, which seemed to be everywhere, were the same. As he grew older he seemed to become more effeminate almost. Meanwhile his wife was increasingly masculine – within a few years of the old King's death she was certainly inviting men to the new house where they would have tea in the afternoon in her rooms with the curtains drawn, just as she had done in the old days.

When we used to clear up after a visit from Lord Alington or one of her rich city friends whom she still saw, it was always clear that they hadn't just sat there sipping tea. I think some of her new men slept with her because they were too frightened to refuse – she was a very big personality, very persuasive. People wanted to do what she wanted them to do.

Meanwhile George kept the curtains open and just liked to giggle and chat with his women friends and he was so meticulous about everything that his room hardly needed tidying afterwards. It was always just so because he was very house-proud in a way that most people at that time associated with women. Mind you, it was marvellous for us maids because Mrs Keppel's rooms were a mess when she finished whereas George's rooms hardly needed any attention. We preferred him really.

Sonia was barely a teenager when Bertie died, but signs of trouble had long been growing around Violet who was eighteen in 1912. No one yet guessed that Violet was homosexual, but she was certainly a rule breaker. She flirted throughout her life with both sexes. As a teenager she had a platonic fling with Julian Grenfell, son of Lady Desborough and her MP husband Henry Grenfell, and she was scolded severely on one occasion after being found in a cupboard with him at Grosvenor Street.

Alice was furious, not because she disliked Grenfell, but because the rule was that unmarried girls could not behave in such a way. She would have explained to Violet that such behaviour would damage her marriage chances – sleeping around was not permitted until after one was married.

On one occasion Agnes Cook overheard a furious row between Violet and her mother:

> We could hear them through the drawing room door. Usually family matters were kept for the bedrooms and Mrs Keppel's private suite – George Keppel rarely got involved in what his daughters did or did not do unless it got really bad as it did much later.

But the day Violet was found with Mr Grenfell there was a terrible row and Alice insisted Violet must at all times be chaperoned when she was with any single men her own age. Violet screamed back at her mother that marriage was horrible and that she, Alice, had treated her husband George abominably – that was the word she used – by seeing other men. Alice then firmly laid down the law that the rules had to be obeyed if Violet wanted to marry well. Violet shouted back that she did not want to marry well.

After a visit to the family home at Duntreath, Violet got into more trouble by falling in love with the porter from the local railway station. She clearly felt that Johnny McPhail was someone untainted by the hypocrisy and deceit of the ruling class to which she belonged. When the young porter sent a love letter to Violet, Alice intercepted it and tore it up. She told Violet that it was impossible to imagine anyone wanting to be the wife of a porter.

The difficulty with Julian Grenfell went away when he was killed in the First World War. Meanwhile Violet got round the problem of being chaperoned with young men by flirting with older men – often the men she had seen her mother flirt (and sleep) with. She also realised very early on – and to her mother's horror – that flirting with young women could hardly be banned since there was no official acknowledgement that such flirting could ever be anything other than friendship.

It was Alice's bizarre moral code that so infuriated Violet. Violet's rapidly developing view was that if love was genuine it should not be hidden behind a wall of secrecy and intrigue, which is why, when she fell for Vita Sackville-West, she seemed almost unconcerned who knew. She hated the idea of secrecy, yet secrecy lay at the heart of her mother's view of how life should be conducted. And just as Bertie and the Marlborough House set thought it was disgraceful for a man to seduce a young unmarried girl (assuming she was not middle or lower class), so Alice felt that no girl should live away from home until safely married – she had to go from the control and supervision of her parents into the control and supervision of her husband. Or at least that was how it had to seem on the surface.

Occasionally and despite her legendary charm, Alice would meet someone who would point out the hypocrisy of her position. When Alice chided the young, unmarried Edith Sitwell for not living with her parents, Edith explained that she had left home because she could not write while living under her parents' roof; it was too stultifying. Alice responded by asking, 'But do you prefer poetry to human love?' Lightning fast the future author of *Façade* shot back: 'As a profession, yes.'

It was a remark that hit home. Alice would have felt the sting of this riposte but no doubt refused to take offence. At the same time the barbed comment would have summed up for Violet Keppel all that was wrong with her mother's view of life.

Like so many English aristocrats who looked back over the long years of Edward VII's reign and that of his mother Queen Victoria, Alice was convinced that, despite the rumour, a European-wide war was impossible. After all, the British royal family was to all intents and purposes German – for a few more years it would still be known as the house of Saxe-Coburg and Gotha, until pressure from the public and government forced George V to change the family name to Windsor, something he hated doing.

So while rumours of war grew, Alice continued the social round with numerous trips abroad to Spain, Holland and France as 1912 slipped into 1913. After her world tour she had skilfully re-established herself in London with an admittedly diminished number of friends compared to the days when she was still part of the royal circle. It was a lesser world it is true, but life was far better than she might have feared in 1910 and with the King only recently dead.

As ever she travelled several times a year with old friends. In Holland she and George were entertained by Lord and Lady Ponsonby and in Spain by the man who had helped turn a small fortune provided for Alice by Bertie into a vast fortune: Sir Ernest Cassel.

But as Agnes Cook recalled, Alice's relationship with Violet was worsening:

> She was always nagging poor Violet and she just couldn't accept that the world was changing and what was good enough for her – Alice I mean – might not be right for Violet. I suppose it happens to everyone – the parents think their rules should last for ever and their children want something different.

Apart from fights with her daughter – which, according to Agnes Cook, continued when the family went abroad – Alice's life was an endless series of lunches in the houses of friends in England and Scotland punctuated by visits to galleries and museums.

When war finally came in August 1914, Alice and George were still in the Netherlands. They were told that they needed to leave for England as quickly as possible, but with the assurance and sense of entitlement of the English upper classes they still managed to leave for Newhaven at a leisurely pace and with their vast store of luggage – more than thirty large trunks – and servants. But what was called the phoney war was soon to turn into a war of such horror that even Alice Keppel must have realised that things were unlikely ever to be the same again.

Back in England the idea took hold that the war would all be over by Christmas and that, for the aristocracy at least, life would then quickly return to normal. Even in the trenches there was an attempt to make sure that the officers had a semblance of life as they had known it at home. These plans were occasionally upset – when, for example, the lorry carrying several tons of the officers' regimental silver got stuck in a muddy ditch in France. Alice was so disgusted by the war that she announced that if she had sons she would ship them off abroad to avoid the carnage. Agnes Cook remembered the atmosphere in the house:

> Well, suddenly all the young male servants, or most of them, disappeared and we women servants were left to get on with it. We all knew that Mrs Keppel thought the war was a lot of nonsense and she said that if she'd had a son she would make him go to Ireland to avoid the risk of being killed. We thought this was a bit unpatriotic

but the family knew several other aristocratic families that had sent their sons to Ireland or Canada for the duration just in case.

Alice's fears about the reality of war were soon to be painfully realised. Two of her nephews, including her brother Archie's son William, were to be killed in France before the war ended, and for the first time in their lives Alice and other members of the governing classes felt the moral pressure to do something to help others rather than simply continue their lives of leisure.

Alice worked for a time in a Red Cross hospital at Étaples doing clerical work, but with no experience of practical work she left after a month and quickly returned to London. Agnes recalled her weariness at this time:

> Oh she hated the war and she hated having to be part of it in any way, but felt she had to do something but it was a token gesture – what did she know about work? Violet was the same and she was so hopeless that she was sacked after making a cup of cocoa for a general using a powder designed to clean knives.

But the social round was sadly diminished as many big country houses were commandeered as hospitals; others found formerly grand families living in reduced circumstances because most of their servants had been called up and they could not do the simplest thing for themselves.

They were reduced to living in one or two rooms entirely at the mercy of an elderly cook or maid. Vita Sackville-West's mother, Lady

Sackville, was probably typical of the English aristocracy when she wrote to Lord Kitchener to complain that it was grossly unfair to deprive her of her servants since this made her usual life impossible:

> I think perhaps you do not realise Lord K, that we employ five carpenters and four painters and two blacksmiths and two footmen and you are taking them all from us. I do not complain about the footmen, although I must say I never thought I would see parlour maids at Knole! I am putting up with them because I know I must, but it really does offend me to see these women hovering around me in their starched aprons, which are not at all what Knole is used to instead of liveries and even powdered hair!
>
> Dear Lord K, I am sure you will sympathise with me when I say that parlour maids are so middle class, not at all what you and I are used to. But as I said that is not what I complain about. What I do mind is your taking all our carpenters from us ... Do you not realise my dear Lord K that you are ruining houses like ours? After all there is Hatfield where Queen Elizabeth spent her time as a young princess and that is historic too, just like Knole, and I am sure Lord Salisbury would tell you he was having frightful difficulties in keeping Hatfield going just as we are having in keeping Knole. What can you do about it? ... do help me all you can.

Lady Sackville also wrote to the Chancellor of the Exchequer Andrew Bonar Law asking for concessions from 'crippling income tax and death duties'. Her attitude to her life and her needs is typical of the view of a section of the English upper classes during the war.

Alice Keppel was perhaps more sensitive than some to the tide of change sweeping the country, but she no doubt also felt that the new world would not be much to her liking. In the past the aristocracy had enjoyed a large measure of deference from the lower classes, but endless criticism now seemed the order of the day.

As one commentator put it in the *The Clarion* newspaper:

> The English aristocracy show their true colours by complaining their parasitical lives cannot continue as before. They think wars are to be fought on their behalf by others as their hearths are kept warm by others, their estates kept going by others. When the finest foods and wines can no longer be got from France, they speak to their friends in the ministry and are baffled at how a war is permitted to interfere with the day-to-day necessaries of a gilded existence.

It was as if a compact had been broken. If the governing class could not prevent this disastrous war, what on earth were they for? Why had the country kept them in cotton wool and luxury for so long when their ability to govern seemed entirely lacking just when it was most needed?

❊←┄❊❊┄→❊

Despite the war, Alice was able to visit friends in France and in 1915 she was in Paris – a visit that suggests that in certain circles the war was still seen as a little local difficulty. From London her two daughters continued their visits to the country houses of friends.

George had volunteered for military service but escaped the oblit-
eration of the bulk of his battalion, the 10th (Service) Battalion of
the Royal Fusiliers, at the Battle of Pozières in 1916 by being posted
to Ireland.

It was turmoil, but the Keppels, even in Ireland, were brilliant at
maintaining a semblance of their old lives – dining out, visiting friends
and enjoying country house weekends. In 1916 Alice stayed for a time
at the home of the Sackvilles at Knole in Kent and then at Buckhurst
Park, home of Earl De La Warr, from where Sonia returned to London in time to celebrate her sixteenth birthday on 31 May.

There were visits to Watlington Park in Oxfordshire and to
Trent Park in Hertfordshire, followed by a stay in Ireland to be
with George Keppel at the Georgian house he had rented for the
family and where they were still served by the ever-faithful butler
Rolfe and other servants.

Agnes Cook remembered this period well:

> The truth is the Keppels would have starved without servants. They
> had no idea how to do anything practical for themselves because they'd
> grown up in a world where doing nothing was seen as a sign of good
> breeding. Even then it seemed to be a mad idea to me!
>
> It was only after the war that more and more working people began
> to feel that the families they had worked for as servants were really
> just hopeless! Looking back now it's almost comical that that was how
> the world was once run. Even George's military career was a bit of
> a joke – he was made a lieutenant colonel simply because he was an
> aristocrat despite having no real military experience; when he left for

Ireland all he was worried about was remembering the silver tongs he used to curl his moustache with. He was a dandy who relied entirely on real soldiers, I mean the rank and file, to do the work and he spent all his time in the officers' mess smoking and talking and eating and drinking just as he did in his club in London.

But there is no doubt the death of Alice's nephew William shocked her deeply and the world that emerged at the end of the war was a world that lacked many of the old certainties of the Edwardian era. Like most middle-aged and elderly people then as in every era, Alice Keppel found it very difficult to accept that the next generation wanted freedoms and modes of life that were alien to her. Indeed, it might be said that through her daughters she fought for the rest of her life to keep the new world at bay.

In the meantime, she continued her afternoon assignations and worried about Violet. She desperately wanted both daughters married into the peerage, and to ensure that they enjoyed the kind of life she had enjoyed. She felt the highest achievement for a woman was the extent to which she was able to use her charm and her wit and her physical beauty to become part of what was then termed 'society', but also to ensure that she became and remained wealthy.

She loathed the idea that women might find other lives as doctors or lawyers or politicians. Of course working-class women had always worked but that was different; the daughters of the aristocracy would, Alice hoped, go on for ever marrying well, visiting each other's grand houses and discussing their own lives in measured patrician tones. For Alice such a life was a supreme achievement and the fact that one of her daughters wanted nothing to do with it was both deeply hurtful and utterly incomprehensible. Violet's refusal to take the route long-established by her mother and numerous other aristocratic women in their circle also had dangerous practical implications.

All her life Alice had acted to make money and avoid scandal and now her daughter was to lead her into years of just the kind of public scandal she had always managed to avoid.

Chapter 13

Love Among the Ruins

ALICE AND GEORGE knew that Violet was not like other girls, to use the sort of euphemism popular in Edwardian England. She had had crushes on a number of girls before the friendship with Vita Sackville-West exploded into full-scale romantic passion, but no doubt Violet's parents felt school-girl crushes would come to an end once Violet became an adult.

But Violet was far more deeply opposed to her mother's world than anyone could have imagined. Despite her later, deeply unhappy marriage, she was to enjoy affairs with, among others, the great Parisian society hostess, Princess de Polignac, but it was Vita Sackville-West who came closest to destroying the delicately balanced world that Violet and her mother inhabited.

Violet first met Vita in 1904. Vita was twelve and Violet ten. Both had typically English upper-class mothers – emotionally detached from their offspring, they relied on servants to bring up their small children and were physically as well as emotionally absent most of the time.

Also both had mothers whose main focus was outside the family. Lady Sackville had lost interest in her husband and was obsessed with Sir John Murray Scott; Alice had been entirely focused on Bertie for much of Violet's teens.

In both cases, money was a large part of the attraction – Lady Sackville eventually inherited millions from Sir John Murray Scott while, as we have seen, Alice Keppel grew rich on the lavish funds supplied by Bertie. But there were differences too – Lady Sackville alternately charmed and humiliated Sir John Scott while Alice only charmed.

The two girls were close from the day they met; indeed for a short time they even went to school together in South Audley Street in Mayfair, and it was at this time that the seeds of one of the great lesbian love affairs of the twentieth century were sown.

As a child Violet shared a set of rooms with her sister Sonia on the top two floors of the big house in Portman Square. It's hard to imagine now, but twenty-four hours a day, seven days a week, the girls were looked after by a maid, a nanny and a governess. So from her earliest years Violet was surrounded by women, and outside the top two floors she would have been aware of her father as a delightful but ineffective presence, someone who survived in the slipstream of her larger-than-life mother. All her life Violet was aware that she did not quite live up to the femine might of her mother. From a material point of view, however, life was idyllic.

Violet enjoyed annual holidays in Biarritz, with Bertie usually staying nearby. And the family travelled in style – the railway company had to be warned in advance, so vast was the pile of boxes and trunks. The Keppel luggage for six weeks in the south of France filled one whole van on the train.

Years later Sonia Keppel published her memoirs and she recalled her mother's less glamorous side. She remembered Alice greasing her face at night in their sleeping berth, putting her hair up in a cap and taking a sleeping pill, a habit she had all her adult life. She also drank heavily – an addiction that was to lead eventually to her death from cirrhosis of the liver.

Violet learned to hate Biarritz – 'callous and trivial', she called it – because their lives there were entirely ruled by the King's whims. Her mother would lunch with the King every day and then walk along the promenade with him arm in arm; then there would be sightseeing and dinner followed by cards. Bertie was an absolute social tyrant. Unlike Violet, Alice had long ago accepted that this was just how it had to be.

Violet was astonished at her mother's brilliance and use of her feminine charms – 'she excelled in making others happy', she wrote – but was also disgusted by her lack of sincerity, her pretence that there was nothing undignified or duplicitous in her behaviour. She probably felt sorry for her father too, who in exchange for money and position was happy to be cuckolded.

Violet was expected to visit various grand houses regularly for tea and it was at one of these – Lady Kilmorey's house just off Park Lane – that she first met Vita. Later on, Vita came to tea at Portman Square. Violet then went to Knole for tea with the Sackvilles. It was all highly decorous on the surface and Alice Keppel was no doubt delighted that her daughter had made friends with a member of one of England's most ancient families.

Looking back many years later, Vita recognised the depth of this early attachment when she wrote, 'there is a bond that unites me to Violet – Violet is mine'. The story of the two women's affair is well known, but Violet's mother's reaction to it, her battle to control what was going on, is central to the second half of Mrs Keppel's life. In fighting to preserve her daughter's conventional existence, Alice was fighting to preserve a world that was already dead. She won the battle but left her daughter's life in ruins.

By 1908, four years after they first met, Violet was professing undying love for Vita. By the time Bertie died and Violet's mother's life was in turmoil, the two girls had almost certainly consummated their affair. Alice Keppel was too distracted by grief at the King's death and the business of thinking what to do next to understand what was happening to her daughter and as a result she misjudged the seriousness of this new relationship.

In 1912, having returned from the Far East, Alice began to plan what she hoped would be a spectacular coming-out ball for her eldest daughter – it was an event that was to mark the first step in the conventional route to marriage.

Three hundred people came to Violet's party but, despite the enormous success of the event, the year wore on without Violet seeming any nearer a good marriage. Alice felt increasingly frustrated that among all the rich aristocratic young men she invited to her house, none seemed to sufficiently interest Violet. But Alice also knew by now that Violet was not behaving in a way that would encourage any suitable young man.

For the truth was that Violet only wanted Vita. Their letters to each other at this time became increasingly passionate and, in Violet's case, reckless. Not for her the calm considered tones of her mother; she wanted full-blown passion and the language of her letters makes this clear.

As early as 1910 she had written:

Well, you ask me point-blank why I love you ... I love you, Vita, because I've fought so hard to win you ... I love you because you have never yielded in anything ... I love you because you never capitulate. I love you for your wonderful intelligence, for your literary aspirations ... I love you because you have the air of doubting nothing ... I love you, Vita, because I have seen your soul.

Vita was not as rebellious as Violet had hoped and her marriage to Harold Nicolson in 1913 almost led to a temporary breach between the two women. Violet was consumed with jealousy and flirted with the idea of marrying several different men, but it was all just an attempt to make Vita jealous. To Violet's mother's increasing horror, her daughter was clearly unable or unwilling to shake off this unholy passion.

Meanwhile Violet's younger sister Sonia, witnessing the seemingly endless shouting matches and scenes of violent emotional battles between her mother and her sister, vowed to do things by the book. From the earliest age she knew that rebellion was not for her and that she would emulate her mother by marrying well and remaining discreet about any affairs she might have. Sonia far more than Violet was Alice Keppel's daughter, as Agnes Cook remembered:

Sonia was quieter, more obedient, than Violet but underneath the calm exterior she was far more ruthless. She would have married a rusty bucket if it had a title, a big country house and a million in the bank. When she later met and married I don't believe for a minute it was for love. She married because her mother approved of the match and there is no doubt she would have taken a series of lovers when the marriage began to fail, but there was no need by then. Because divorce had become socially acceptable, Sonia didn't have to do as her mother did – I mean sleep around while pretending to be happily married. Like her daughter Rosalind and her granddaughter Camilla, she could get divorced, re-marry and then sleep around. All this lesbianism was horrible for Mrs Keppel.

Meanwhile the battles with Violet continued, as Agnes explains:

For years, almost a decade until 1922 I think, things were awful for Mrs Keppel. She almost had a nervous breakdown because Violet was

always running off with unsuitable girls and her mother knew she was
having sex with them, especially Vita. And Alice hated it when she
could not control everyone around her – George, Archie and Sonia
had always done as they were told. Why couldn't Violet?

Major Denys Trefusis, a descendant of Lord Clinton, must have
seemed a godsend to Alice. He was good-looking and a major in
the Royal Horse Guards with a distinguished war record. Alice must
have sensed that, like her own husband, Denys was likely to be a
mild-mannered, complaisant husband – something Violet also recognised as she flirted with him at parties and in letters as 1918 wore on.

Under enormous pressure from Alice, Violet agreed to marry
Denys, but the Keppels were so worried by their unstable daughter
that, in the months leading up to the wedding, Violet was never left
alone at Grosvenor Street nor allowed out unaccompanied.

Alice told Violet that Denys would be unlikely to stop her affair
with Vita and that marriage would make it easier for Violet to live
as she pleased. But marriage was also perhaps Violet's way of getting her revenge on Vita for marrying Harold. Why Denys wanted
to marry someone who made it clear before their marriage that she
did not care for him is a mystery. It was almost as if, despite his
later tears and rages, he enjoyed being abused. But whatever their
deeper thoughts and feelings, Violet and Denys were married at the
Grosvenor Chapel in Mayfair on 16 June 1919.

Alice brought the full weight of her money and her social connections down on the wedding – no expense was spared. Hundreds were
invited, there were heaps of gold and silver wedding presents and an

extraordinary sumptuous lunch. Even the servants at Grosvenor Street were dragooned into clubbing together to buy a silver inkstand for the couple – 'We hated doing it because we were poor as church mice, but we felt we had to do it to keep our jobs,' recalled Agnes.

But the marriage was a sham. Violet continued to see Vita and would have little to do with Denys. Soon the whole extended family and, worse, their friends, got to know about the affair. But the marriage so upset Vita that she kidnapped Violet from what was supposed to be her honeymoon suite at the Ritz and virtually raped her. She later wrote in her diary: 'I treated her savagely, I made love to her, I had her, I didn't care, I only wanted to hurt Denys.'

The family knew all about this because Violet told her mother deliberately to taunt her with her lesbianism. Sonia, Alice and George were horrified, not because Violet wanted to have sex with women but because people might find out, as Agnes explains: 'I know for a fact that Alice said again and again to Violet that it was fine for her to sleep with women while she was married, so long as she remained married and made it clear to the world that she was living with her husband.'

Alice's immense power over her daughter was not easily overthrown, especially since Violet was incapable of making a cup of tea and had no money beyond that supplied by her mother. She was trapped and she knew it.

Even Vita, who was never quite as committed to the relationship as Violet was, wrote that she felt translated or reborn by sex with Violet.

Violet herself wrote that on a holiday they'd enjoyed in Cornwall in 1918, she and Vita 'sometimes … loved each other so much we became inarticulate'. It was passion without guile and beyond reason that Violet wanted, and now she had it. Her mother's attempt to impose a calculated response to love had been jettisoned for an affair that had no rational bounds.

Alice's response again and again was to insist that Violet must maintain the outward show of her marriage – otherwise she could do as she pleased. But Violet wanted to shout her love to the world rather than slip unnoticed through the old hypocritical paths her mother frequented. Her desire for freedom even extended to going out with Vita dressed as a man – and they stayed in hotels in the guise of a young newly married couple. It was a deceit, but a deceit a million miles from what Violet saw as the tawdry deceits of her mother. It was genuine love and genuine romance.

For months at a time, Violet wrote five or six letters a day to Vita and eventually begged her to agree to run away with her and live together permanently in France. It was a childhood fantasy of escape, from husbands, from mothers, from the old world of bad faith. Meanwhile Vita told her husband Harold she had no intention of leaving him and just asked him to be patient while she enjoyed her passionate interlude.

By 1920, London was awash with gossip about Violet's passion for Vita and Alice was determined to put a stop to it.

The story of Violet Keppel's engagement and marriage, of her affair with Vita and its consequences has been told many times, either from Violet's point of view or from Vita's; Alice Keppel's life during this period has been less well understood. We know it was a period of sustained anxiety lest, through her daughter, she should lose the social world which had been badly shaken by the death of Edward VII. The friends she had retained after the death of Edward VII would stick by her, but only so far; if the scandal surrounding Violet and Vita reached the newspapers or, worse, the divorce courts, Alice would be ostracised, or at least that was Alice's fear.

Agnes Cook describes a house at war with itself:

Well, the problem was that Violet was an adult who in theory could do as she pleased, but Alice was having none of that. She dragged Violet from country house to country house to keep her away from Vita in the run up to Violet's wedding. But it all ended in farce because, both before and after the marriage, Vita and Violet met whenever they could sneak away from their partners. Mind you, Violet didn't really sneak away at all – she threw her affair in poor Denys's face, but then he was a dry old stick. Very conventional and reserved. He'd been through a terrible war, but from what we heard it was not nearly as bad as his war with Violet, which went on for ten years – from 1919 when they married until 1929 when he died of tuberculosis.

What made us laugh was that when Vita married she didn't mind that Violet was upset, but when Violet married Denys, Vita was furious. Or at least that was the rumour flying about the house. I read about it years later and realised that those rumours had been spot on. At the time we servants just thought – don't these people have anything better to do? It all came from having too much money and too little to do and too much to think about!

In fact, it was Violet's marriage and arguments about whether or not it had been consummated that were to lead eventually to the end of Vita and Violet's affair and victory for Alice Keppel.

The whole business was complicated by Vita's husband Harold, who could hardly seek to control his wife when he himself had homosexual affairs throughout his marriage. Alice Keppel found it impossible to control her daughter for similar reasons – she could hardly appeal to Violet on moral grounds since her own adult life had been characterised by immorality of a similar kind.

In the salons of Mayfair the buzz of gossip must have been profoundly upsetting as people whispered about Violet and said the marriage could not possibly last and that Violet was a 'disgusting Sapphist'.

Even with Violet married, the whiff of scandal might've been enough, not only to ruin Alice's life, but also that of her second daughter, who had yet to find a suitably advantageous marriage. In fact, these fears were well founded and Violet's affair with Vita was almost to scupper Sonia's chances.

From the start of their marriage, Denys and Violet were deeply unhappy. They rowed and fought continually. Alice simply thought they were not handling matters properly. She could not see why passion should interfere with the rules of society.

Within weeks of the marriage, Alice was begging her mother to be allowed to leave her new husband. Alice appears to have hinted that if Violet did this she would be cut off without a penny. That was at last something that Violet understood. So the marriage lurched on from one shouting match to another with Violet constantly seeing Vita, and Denys snubbed at every turn.

By now Alice's life was in turmoil. She was drinking heavily and taking increasing quantities of drugs to help her sleep. The greatest threat was to her second daughter Sonia who had met and hoped to marry one of the richest young men in England, Roland Cubitt, whose grandfather had founded the firm that built most of Belgravia.

Alice had no objections to Cubitt's tradesman origins. Roland was rich and that was all that mattered. He was also due to inherit the title Lord Ashcombe on the death of his father. But rumours about a lesbian sister had already reached Roland's parents, who were devout. Indeed they made it very clear from the outset that they disapproved of their son's choice and not just because of Violet's behaviour – they also hated Alice's past as the King's mistress.

Alice put Violet under what effectively amounted to house arrest while negotiations for Sonia's marriage got underway. She was able to write a few letters to Vita but she was not allowed to see her. Meanwhile Denys had given up trying to persuade Violet to live with him, and Vita and Violet planned to escape together to Paris.

Alice told Denys he must collect Violet from Paris and take her to a small house she had rented near Tunbridge Wells. It was a mad plan. Vita allowed Violet to believe they might be together for ever, even as she planned to return to Harold. Violet retreated to Tunbridge Wells, where Denys and her mother begged her to be reasonable.

Even the normally torpid George Keppel sprang into action, so horrified was he by the events of 1920 – but the end of Violet's affair with Vita came at last when, in an extraordinary series of events that have been told and retold, Alice rented a light aircraft and made

Denys and Harold pilot it to France to drag their wives back – by force if necessary.

After a turbulent meeting at a hotel in Amiens, Vita agreed to return to her husband. Harold had convinced Vita that Violet had broken her word and consummated her marriage to Denys. It was probably untrue but it gave Vita a way out. She told Violet they must separate for two months but it was in reality the end of their affair and the end of all Violet's hopes that they might elope and live together for ever as a couple.

Violet was judged harshly throughout the long progress of her affair with Vita; this was inevitable because, though the world to which she and her mother belonged would countenance any number of heterosexual affairs, homosexuality, especially between women, was beyond the pale.

Sibyl Colefax, who knew Violet well later in life, described her as 'good company but really wicked'. In his memoirs, Harold Acton, who knew Violet in her years of exile in Florence, said she was 'perhaps the most selfish woman I have known – so selfish and inconsiderate she became a joke'.

Of course, Acton was famously malicious and his comments have to be taken with a pinch of salt as he was unkind about almost everyone, but a pattern does emerge. Violet was wilful in a way that must have astonished her mother, but in fact her desire to control her world and do just as she pleased was not that different from Alice's own need to dominate.

Violet's sister Sonia said that Violet had always been an adult – meaning probably that the adult Violet was exactly the same as the child Violet: petulant, impetuous, fanatical, jealous and dangerously high-spirited.

Where Alice loved for money, Violet loved for its own sake and had an almost pathological need to flirt – just as her mother had always done. She was certainly deeply in love with Vita throughout the period of their relationship, but at the same time she continued to flirt outrageously with anyone, male or female, she met and liked.

The truth about Violet is that she was never wholly serious except about Vita and the ultimate failure of that affair seeped so deeply into her personality that she never really recovered from it. The rest of her life was a lament for what had been lost. All her novels – she wrote and published seven – are barely concealed attempts to relive and to make sense of her affair with Vita.

Though deeply disturbed by the turmoil of her daughter's life, Alice fought back against the gossips.

When Lady Sackville spoke publicly of her daughter's friend being a 'sexual pervert', Alice made clear her own view of Lady Sackville. To anyone who would listen she pointed out that Lady Sackville's own private life would not stand up to scrutiny – she had had a long, if platonic, affair with Sir John Murray Scott and had ended up in the courts in a row about his money. She was also considered eccentric to say the least.

But the scandal and the worries about Sonia and, increasingly, about money were taking their toll. An old friend of Violet's called Pat Dansey saw Alice in the distance alone at a table at the casino in Biarritz. She wrote to Violet: 'I saw your mother in the casino yesterday – she does look so ill – worried and sad. And she is quite miserable over the whole beastly business.'

And she asks: 'Cannot anything be done to arrange things without this horrible disgrace?'

Things had been done but Violet could never stick to an agreement. Alice was baffled that her daughter would not do the right thing – she had offered to pay for Violet and Denys to go away for a year on a trip around the world, or they could stay with her friend, the painter Sir John Lavery in Tangier; anything to avoid what Pat Dansey called 'this fire of hateful gossip'.

Having failed to persuade Violet to be reasonable, Alice focused on Denys. She told him that if he ever separated from Violet she would give her daughter £600 a year and not a penny more – ever. She would never see her again or allow her to come to the house in Grosvenor Street. When the message reached Violet via Denys she seems to have realised, finally, that she really was on the brink of penury.

Alice implied that once Sonia was safely married, Violet and Denys could do as they pleased – so long as they did not divorce. Roland Cubitt's father had made it clear that he hated the idea of his son, who was now Sonia's fiancé, marrying the daughter of 'little Mrs George'. But Roland was smitten and it would take more than Mrs Keppel's by now ancient royal connections to put him off. Lord Ashcombe decided to discuss the marriage settlement with Violet's father.

Alice Keppel's real power can nowhere better be judged than by the fact that when Lord Ashcombe arrived at 16 Grosvenor Street, he was ushered into Alice's presence, not George's. Alice quickly made it clear that any discussion would be with her and not with her husband. Ashcombe was thrown off his guard.

Taking the initiative Alice suggested the Ashcombes should give their son an amount equal to the sum Alice was prepared to give Sonia. As a gentleman faced with such a proposal from a lady, Ashcombe had no choice but to agree, but he was shocked at the huge sum proposed.

It was a cunning move, and typical of Alice. She had fallen out of love with Violet, who had always been the favoured daughter, and this was a way of rewarding Sonia for obeying the rules. A generous dowry also made it more difficult for Ashcombe to justify trying to stop the marriage.

Sonia was delighted at the outcome – the obedient, buck-toothed daughter didn't have her mother's looks, but she shared her desire to be rich and well connected. Where Violet was a wild romantic, Sonia wanted to live life at the highest social level.

Meanwhile, negotiations with Violet continued and after her daughter threatened suicide Alice reluctantly agreed that she would accept an annulment of Violet and Denys's marriage, but only if Violet then agreed to live abroad for at least five years.

❊⟶❊❊⟵❊

By the time rumour had turned into acknowledged fact, everyone who was anyone in London knew that 'little Mrs George's' daughter's marriage was effectively over. Denys Trefusis had returned to the family home in the West Country to be nursed by his mother, and Violet was up to her old Sapphist tricks. Denys, defeated and almost certainly clinically depressed, was ill with the tuberculosis that was soon to kill him. But Sonia at least was now safely married and pregnant with her first child.

The whole Keppel family was determined to keep Violet out of the country – her uncle Archie berated her for hours, her father refused to speak to her unless she agreed to go into exile and Alice refused to allow her to come to the south of France to be with her. Even Violet's maid and former governess had, it seemed, turned against her. The family accepted that the marriage was over but Violet must simply go away.

Agnes Cook recalled how even the servants sensed that the family was in turmoil:

It was really strained. Mrs Keppel could not conceal her upset and anxiety from anyone. It was almost as bad as when the King died. She hated to be talked about at dinner parties across London and I think as a result she always imagined the gossip was worse than it really was – but she was determined that Violet should do as she was told. They didn't want her in England; it was too embarrassing, so when she turned up she was locked up! Even the butler Rolfe had been told to take control of Violet if she insisted on coming to the house. He had been instructed to open all her letters and to give them to George Keppel to be destroyed – just in case they were from Vita Sackville-West. Even the humblest servant in the house like me knew that Violet was in disgrace, but there was something so impulsive about her that whatever anyone said or did, whatever the threats, she refused to back down. When her mother said she'd get no money that frightened Violet and she would knuckle under for a while, and then when things got quiet she'd start off again.

We thought that, like her mother, Violet was just sex-obsessed – she managed to sneak Mrs Nicolson, Vita Sackville-West that is – into the house in Grosvenor Street on a number of occasions when her mother was away. You can only really lock someone up if you are around to keep an eye on them. And Mrs Keppel hated to be tied down. She loved the gambling tables of the south of France and couldn't bear to be away from them for long, even if her daughter was causing terrible trouble.

We regularly saw Mrs Nicolson go up to Violet's apartments and stay there all night long after their affair was supposed to be over. That's what made Alice so wild – her daughter would give the impression that she would behave and then at the first opportunity she'd be at it again. Violet really was the ultimate spoilt child.

Violet never lost her inability to cope with anything practical. When she was evacuated from France at the start of the Second World War, she handed all her jewellery to a man on the ship, simply assuming he was a porter. She assumed everyone around her who was not of her class was there to sort things for her. Sonia was far better at coping with the real world.

Agnes Cook again:

Sonia wanted society and wanted a rich marriage and even if the Cubitts were not quite top drawer – they were just rich builders

– money by now was the main thing. Status was great but money was more important. Especially as Mrs Keppel was always aware that she herself was tarnished, however carefully she pretended that was not the case.

In the event the marriage between Denys and Violet was never annulled. Having tried living together in various places just to keep Alice from refusing to give them any more money, they ended up in a flat in Paris but rarely saw each other. Each carried on affairs with other people throughout the 1920s and Alice ensured the couple had enough money to distract them from the horror of their nominal alliance.

With Sonia safely married and Violet permanently exiled to France, Alice and George continued to visit the country houses of their friends. The now rather diminished lunches continued at Grosvenor Street and there were regular trips to the south of France and even a cruise to the Near East. But for Alice the London of the 1920s was unappealing. Taxes only mooted while Bertie was alive had long eaten away at the fortunes of the old landed aristocracy and many of the great London houses that Alice had known as a young woman were being demolished to make way for offices and flats. Devonshire House in Piccadilly, one of the great centres of social life before the war, came down in 1927.

Stuck with Denys, and with Vita to all intents and purposes gone, Violet reconciled herself to life in permanent exile. She wrote in her autobiography that she had thought Paris would make up for everything, and to some extent it did, for it had always been far more tolerant of homosexuality and unconventional life in general than England had ever been.

She fell in love with the immensely rich Princess de Polignac. True it was a lesbian affair, but even Alice approved as Violet had at least had the decency to choose a Princess this time – and an immensely wealthy one at that.

To Alice's relief, the end of her daughter's affair with Vita Sackville-West meant gossip in London began to subside. Defeated in love, Violet began to resemble her mother more and more. She now played by the rules, rarely returned to London, kept her affair with the Princess as discreet as possible, mixed almost every evening in the most aristocratic circles and entertained on a level that compared favourably with her mother's glory days in Portman Square. Violet bought a house at Auteuil in 1923 and turned it into what one friend, the painter Jaques-Émile Blanche described as 'a miniature Ritz'. The Ritz had always been one of her mother's favourite hotels.

Always accommodating so long as the surface rules were obeyed, Alice and George even ventured on a cruise with their daughter, accompanied by the Princess de Polignac and even Denys. Perhaps at some level they were all unhappy but they were now too weary to continue to fight each other.

Chapter 14

Among the Exiles

*I*NCREASINGLY UNCOMFORTABLE IN a London now dominated by a younger genera-tion whose values and behaviour seemed baffling, Alice and George began to consider other options. What was there now to keep them in a city where the circles in which they moved were constantly diminishing? They bought a series of large cars and tried to adapt, but Alice secretly longed for the leisured days of drives in the brougham in the park. She also disliked the new unchaperoned dances influenced by American jazz.

Royal circles were now firmly closed to the Keppels. George V would have nothing to do with a woman he believed was responsible for making his mother unhappy; he also despised her for reminding him of his father's lifestyle. But King George could never completely shake Mrs Keppel off. He would have known that, years later when she returned to London for a few weeks at a time from her exile in Italy, she always stayed at the Ritz and always in a suite of rooms that looked directly down at Buckingham Palace where once she had been able to drive in her fashionable carriage through the gates.

Other changes were also unwelcome – many landed families disappeared from London at this time as death duties and falling agricultural prices made estates unviable. New money made by American industrialists and bankers began increasingly to supplant ancient families with little cash to spare. It all seemed a sad decline to George and Alice and they began to plan to leave England for good.

They leased the magnificent house in Grosvenor Street to James Corrigan, an American steel magnate. According to Kirsty McLeod in her book *A Passion for Friendship*, Sibyl Colefax and her circle said that Mrs Corrigan complained about Alice's Keppel's magnificent Chippendale chairs (if indeed they really were by Chippendale). She insisted they were rather vulgar.

But Alice had her revenge. Ever a genius for making money, she charged the Corrigans far more than the lease was worth. In return for the overpayment she handed over a list of the names and addresses of those London aristocrats who habitually came to Grosvenor Street for lunch or dinner. Poor Rolfe, the Keppel's long-serving butler, was also thrown into the bargain.

Agnes Cook remembered what might best be described as the beginning of the end:

After the lease was sold in 1924, the Keppels never returned to Grosvenor Street. I remember the last few months they were there – it had settled into a pattern and Alice Keppel had a routine that must have seemed, if not quite as good as her days with the King, then a pretty good substitute. Various bankers, including I think one of the Rothschilds, came in the afternoons and slept with her, or at least disappeared into her rooms and came out looking very satisfied with themselves.

But these visits were not as frenzied or frequent as they had been in the early years and in the years after she returned from Ceylon and China after King Edward died. I heard later that her flirting and sleeping with people largely came to an end when she went to Italy finally, but she was in her sixties by then so perhaps it's not so surprising.

I left the Corrigans, who'd taken over the Grosvenor Street house, after a year or so – couldn't stand them! – and worked for an English landowner and farmer from East Anglia, but I didn't like the change. He was pompous and rude and difficult to work for because he thought so highly of himself. He was a member of the King's Honourable Corps of Gentlemen at Arms, a sort of personal bodyguard, but made up entirely of pompous dim-witted old buffers with nothing better to do than suck up to the royals. Alice Keppel was at least the real thing and she was never pompous. This new chap wasn't used to London and he was a dim military type, who, having left the army, had been offered a job with the King and, boy, he never let us forget it.

Alice's decision to move to Italy was perhaps not so surprising. For years the Keppels had spent months abroad each year, either touring or on cruises in the Mediterranean or staying with friends in France and Italy or gambling at the casinos in the south of France.

As she grew older, Alice also began to hate the London winters. She persuaded – 'told' might be a better word – George that they should buy a house in Italy and make that their base. They chose an enormous villa on a hill overlooking Florence where they hoped to recreate the style they had enjoyed in London in happier days, but away from gossips who still remembered Violet's disgrace or made jokes about Edward VII's 'loose box'.

The Villa dell'Ombrellino was a palace in all but name. Perched on top of the Bellosguardo – the name means 'beautiful view' – the Ombrellino was said to have once been the home of Galileo. It was a boast that Alice made regularly to visitors. The house was surrounded by magnificent gardens and the principal rooms enjoyed views right across Florence.

Alice chose the house carefully. The mainspring of her life, even into old age, was to give lunches and dinners, to meet people and to entertain; with the right house here in Italy she could dine and gossip with old friends of her generation, many of whom had now also left London to live more or less permanently in warmer southern climes.

In a manner that now seems absurd, cities and towns across Europe could become popular with the English simply because the monarch had visited them once or twice. This was the case with Florence. Queen Victoria had given it the seal of approval by visiting the city on several occasions and pronouncing it tolerable; inevitably she was followed by the English aristocracy desperate to go wherever the Queen led.

Florence continued to be fashionable through Edward VII's reign and into the reign of George V. The fact that Alice and other English expatriates never learned Italian was not an impediment to life because, as Alice realised, she would only ever mix with the English and perhaps a few exiled Russian aristocrats. But it was the exiled English who were to provide the solid base for what Alice hoped would be a life of entertaining, conversation and cards. Without entertaining, as Harold Acton said of Alice, she had nothing but despair.

Alice had in a sense triumphed at last. As a result of her decade and more in Edward VII's bed, she had enough money to buy the Ombrellino outright and to live there in almost medieval splendour. Vast amounts of her London furniture were shipped out – the porcelain she had bought in China, the gifts from Bertie, some of which were said to have been stolen by Bertie from the Brighton Pavilion – and the mementoes of the great love of her life: photographs of the dead King and of Queen Alexandra were everywhere in the new house.

Alice still dressed and undressed four times a day and her clothes were laid out each day by her long-suffering maid, who still wound her wristwatches (including her dress watch for evening wear) and scented her bathwater. No one was allowed to forget that Alice had once been *la favourite* and among the locals her reputed wealth had a dazzling effect. It was quickly agreed that Alice Keppel was one of the richest women in Europe – and she was. But if this kind of gossip was harmless, other comments were hurtful. Everyone knew that Alice had once been the King's mistress and George quickly became known as 'Signor Cuckold'.

Alice's ties to London were too strong to be entirely broken, however, so she organised and paid for a suite of rooms at the Ritz to be kept permanently available for her throughout the year. The cost would have been astronomical, but then she was astronomically rich.

Osbert Sitwell, who liked Alice and stayed at the Ombrellino on many occasions, noticed how the house was a 'piece of Edwardian England transplanted to Italy'. Alice's other guests included Nancy Astor, the Duke of Westminster, Lord Rosebery, Lord Ilchester and the ever-faithful Lord Stavordale, among others. Many were survivors from the Marlborough House days.

But there were younger visitors too. Winston Churchill stayed and painted on the magnificent terrace. And from across Europe came now-shabby Princes and Princesses who had lost or were soon to lose their realms. Chief among these was King Zog, the King of Albania, along with Princess Helen of Greece.

Alice also invited young debutantes sent out to Florence to imbibe Renaissance culture, and the sons and daughters of the Italian aristocracy were always welcome. They all had English governesses and sounded more English than the English.

Alice's genius for keeping up with her friends went back decades and the sons and daughters of those she had charmed at Edward

VII's table knew her and were always made welcome. They had spent their summers in Europe, spoke fluent French and German and were part of that group inspired by Edward VII himself. They were internationalists – as was Alice herself.

The English network, centred in Paris and Florence, that Alice helped create and sustain, lasted until the Second World War. When she was forced to return to London in 1940, Alice always assumed she would be able to pick up the threads of her Italian life when the war was over. Alice was never going to change. Osbert Sitwell said in 1930 that Alice was arrogantly conscious of a role she had to play, but what Sitwell perhaps forgot was that this was the only role Alice knew how to play – there was nothing fake about it; it was the real Alice.

Alice did create a brilliant social life in Florence, but she was less successful at trying to recreate a political salon that had real influence. She still entertained politicians but her advice on international matters was no longer taken seriously. That she still tried to influence the political world was simply evidence that she was living in the past.

Sir Henry Channon, the Conservative MP, wrote in his diary after a visit that 'Alice could not resist inventing and lying' – he meant that she told stories to amuse or impress or to entertain without regard to the truth, and part of this was exaggerating her influence in British political affairs.

Winston Churchill agreed that she simply could not change the habit of a lifetime, and indeed for the rest of her life she gave advice in a charming way and her audience was usually too polite to tell her that her views were out of date; they belonged to the world as it had been in 1900.

Stories about Alice became the stuff of legend. Many were probably apocryphal but they attached to her because she'd always had the reputation of a great talker. And she could still be very amusing. Eddie Marsh, private secretary to Winston Churchill, recalled Alice's talk about a friend of hers who had been painted by Picasso. Alice described how the friend tried to cross the border from Spain into France and was turned back. The friend was baffled until a border guard explained that he couldn't let her into the country carrying a plan of the military defences of Madrid – he was referring to the cubist portrait.

But there were jibes against Alice too. At the outbreak of the Second World War she left France by Royal Navy troopship. She was the only passenger given a cabin and she was treated like royalty, but back in England she liked to give the impression she had been dicing with death on her perilous journey home. She stayed for a while at Polesden Lacey in Surrey. Alice's host, Margaret Greville, listened at great length to Alice's tales of her narrow escape from war-torn Europe, but later said: 'From the way she talked one would think she had swum the Channel with her maid between her teeth.'

Most people in Italy did not laugh at Alice. She was too rich and too regal, but George was not so lucky, perhaps because the Italians took a very dim view of ineffectual men – men who were happy to be cuckolds – and George's years as the complaisant husband of the King's mistress were well known, even in Florence. It was also clear, as it had always been, that Alice ran their lives – in halting Italian she ordered flowers from the gardener, she organised the parties, supervised the menus, dictated the tone of the long lunches and dinners to which invitations were always issued in her name.

But George, floating vaguely as ever in the background, did find a sort of life in Italy. He had separate rooms in the Ombrellino and filled them, as he had in London, with photographs of young women. He had developed a keen interest, or so he said, in the relatively new art of photography. He rented a photographic studio in a side street in the heart of Florence and to this he would invite young women he had picked up in the city's cafés. He would then ask them to take their clothes off to be photographed. Most refused and gradually George's reputation worsened, but he never gave up and never seemed bored. He still had his silver hair brushes – two sets – and the tiny silver tongs with which he curled his now long out of fashion moustaches every day.

Someone who knew nothing of the Keppels' past was invited to lunch one day and when he heard that George's name was Keppel he said: 'How extraordinary that you should have the same name as the late King's mistress!' George, as ever, was unperturbed. Privately, he kept himself busy writing two books of 'contemporary dates' of French and Dutch Painters. This was perhaps in keeping with his old obsession with order, and both books were subtitled 'An Aid To Memory'.

After years of virtual estrangement, Alice was now reconciled with Violet. Sonia had never been a problem but then Sonia had never been the favourite and her rebellion was to come later, when it no longer mattered, with her divorce and remarriage. Alice's wayward elder daughter had now once more become the favourite. After Denys's death in 1929 Violet could do as she pleased with whomsoever she pleased, especially since she now spent almost no time at all in England.

Through her long years in Italy, Alice wrote regular, deeply affectionate letters to Violet saying she could not bear to live without her, and Violet reciprocated signing herself 'Titten'. Alice wrote, 'You are the person I love best in the world.' Odd, perhaps, for a woman who had threatened to cut her daughter off without a penny, but the endearments, no doubt, reflected Alice's guilt that she had destroyed any chance Violet might have had of happiness.

If Sonia thought Violet had always been an adult, the truth was otherwise. In fact, she was the child who never grew up and now in middle age she had reverted to childhood, at least in her relations with her mother.

Violet realised that though the great love of her life had been destroyed by the intolerable pressure to obey society's rules, she could at least console herself with her mother's wealth and connections; she could speak four languages, owned a splendid medieval tower and a house in France. If she could accept the need to live without love and without Vita in particular, she could at least survive.

Violet liked to tease her mother that she was always on the brink of remarrying, and at first Alice believed and feared that this really might happen. She was worried that Violet's suitors were fortune hunters – she warned one that under English law widows did not receive money from their parents if they remarried – but Alice soon realised that Violet's relationships rarely amounted to more than flirtations, and the men she flirted with were almost always homosexual. It was a repeat of Violet's teen years when she flirted outrageously with everyone.

After escaping from France in July 1940, Alice stayed at the Ritz in Piccadilly for the duration of the war; she complained bitterly about the lack of the sort of food she was used to and of the difficulty of finding servants who were not expensive. She was indignant when her long-serving lady's maid asked for a holiday – her first ever – but knowing servants were hard to come by she was too frightened to forbid it. Her maid's temporary replacement was unsatisfactory, for, as Alice said, 'The little fool does not even wind my watches.'

Bored with life at the Ritz, Alice occasionally trooped imperiously across the road for lunch or dinner at the Blue Posts, a pub. Increasingly she worried about her money and became convinced she was on the verge of bankruptcy. As her money was held in banks across Europe, wartime was particularly stressful.

Her old style had not entirely deserted her and at the Ritz she behaved as if she owned the place. She held cocktail parties and invited the few old friends who had remained in or returned to London. But they were all ghosts now from a world that had almost vanished. A journalist writing in the *Daily Mail* unkindly said that denizens of the Ritz were hardly aware there was a war on. He said:

'I saw the King's father's now rather elderly mistress in the Edwardian lounge, looking as if she had forgotten which decade she was living in. She sat bolt upright, smoking an elegant cigarette and appeared as if waiting for her royal lover to arrive any minute.'

Violet was an occasional visitor to the Ritz and there were sufficient friends from Florence to keep some sort of social life going.
But Alice desperately wanted to return to the Ombrellino, partly
because she was terrified the Germans would steal all her things and
partly because decades of smoking and heavy drinking had weakened
her system. The cold, foggy London winters had taken their toll.
She had an almost permanent cough and, like many heavy drinkers,
she began to lose weight.

She tried occasional visits to Violet, who stayed for a while at
Coker Court in Somerset, but the countryside bored her and the
food was even worse than in London. She wrote endless letters to
Violet trying to stop her spending money and claimed to everyone
she met that she was on the verge of destitution. In fact, she was
still astonishingly well off. Worrying about money was simply dis-
placed anxiety about her disrupted life and she was bored. Despite
her best efforts, her cocktail parties at the Ritz were pale imitations
of what she had once been part of.

For both Alice and Violet, England and all it represented had
died and they were desperate to be gone. Both were waiting for the
war to end and for their money and houses in Europe to become
available again.

Sonia was less often visited by Alice. She had always been a more
distant figure who went her own way. She was living in the country,
although rumour had it that her marriage was failing. The couple
divorced in fact in 1947, by which time Alice was dead.

As the war drew to its close, Alice's heavy drinking and drug-
taking – she was permanently tipsy, noted one visitor to the Ritz

– had taken their toll along with her smoking. She was clearly fading. The journalist John Roberston Scott, who met her at this time, recalled her saying: 'I really don't mind what happens just so long as this beastly war ends. There is nothing for me in London and I want my last years – and I don't have many – to be in the sun and with the right sort of people.'

She visited Bournemouth with her brother Archie – they had always remained close – hoping that sea air would ease her endless coughing.

In 1946 she made her way back to Florence, having circumvented currency restrictions that prevented people taking more than £75 out of the country. She used her influence and was allowed to take £500, telling an official that a woman of her background could not be expected to survive as ordinary people survived. She needed a considerable sum just to pay her servants' wages, she said.

On her way to Florence she stopped at Aix to take the cure, but the days spent bathing and resting did little to alleviate her chronic backache and cough and, worryingly, she continued to lose weight.

By that autumn of 1946, Alice and George – carrying boxes of Alice's favourite cigarettes – were back in Florence. The house had been neglected but not badly damaged. Alice immediately set about repairing and redecorating and the works were so extensive she felt she could not live at the house while they were being carried out. She returned to London for Christmas.

In the spring of 1947 she returned to Florence, but by then she knew she was dying. Her doctors in London and Italy told her she was suffering from advanced cirrhosis of the liver brought on by years of heavy drinking. She never complained and never seemed afraid as her life moved towards its end. She died in her grand bedroom looking out over Florence on 11 September 1947. She was seventy-nine.

Now rudderless and alone, George Keppel died just two months later back in London in the suite at the Ritz that his wife had kept on even after the war ended. Taken back to Italy, George was interred with Alice at the Protestant cemetery, Cimitero degli Allori. Neither of the Keppel children seemed particularly upset. Violet had been devoted to her mother in later life, but could not forget how she had once forced her to abandon Vita and marry Denys. Sonia, always more remote, had her own life and impending divorce to contend with.

And Sonia had other concerns, for her daughter Rosalind was soon to give birth to her first child. Camilla, the present wife of the Prince of Wales, was born on 17 July 1947. Camilla grew up to recreate almost precisely the life that her great-grandmother had created, becoming the long-term mistress of another Prince of Wales. She was also baffled no doubt that Diana, Princess of Wales should object to her affair with her husband.

When Alice Keppel died, the real nature of the family dynamic was revealed. Sonia Keppel wrote immediately to her sister saying that all their mother's things must be sold. Violet protested that when Alice had bequeathed the house in Italy to her she cannot possibly have meant that she should have the house but with nothing in it. Sonia was unmoved and told Violet that if she wanted the furniture and pictures she would have to buy them back when they were sold at auction.

Perhaps this was Sonia's way of getting her revenge on the favoured sibling; certainly Alice and both her daughters had learned to put money before other considerations. Whatever her reasons, Sonia was determined to get every penny she could. She was probably furious too that Violet had been left the Ombrellino.

Sonia died aged eighty-six in 1986. She never became Baroness Ashcombe because she divorced Roland Cubitt in 1947, a short while before he inherited the title.

Violet stayed on at the Ombrellino but the house seemed shabby now and half empty. She was often drunk and she acted out a macabre, decayed version of her mother's life. Visitors still came to the house and there were parties, but Violet seemed lost and lonely and, as one friend put it, she seemed just to be going through the motions. It was as if, said Harold Acton, she was merely the ghost of her mother and the house a ghost of the Edwardian world that none of them had ever really escaped. Towards the end of her life, Violet took drugs to make her sleep and drugs to wake her up. She died in 1972, still lost in bitter regrets about the past. She wrote: 'Across my life only one word will be written: waste.' Alice would have found such a sentiment incomprehensible; instead, she would no doubt have echoed Hilaire Belloc's sentiments when he wrote:

'I'm tired of love, I'm still more tired of rhyme
But money gives me pleasure all the time.'

Acknowledgements

I OWE AN ENORMOUS debt to the many historians and biographers who have written about Edward VII, Queen Victoria and their circle, not to mention the royal family in general. Works I have consulted include Jane Ridley's brilliant study, *Bertie: A Life of Edward VII*; A. N. Wilson's *The Victorians* and *Victoria: A Life*; Christopher Hibbert's *Edward VII*; Hugh Evelyn Wortham's *Edward VII, Man and King*; Michael Paterson's *A Brief History of Life in Victorian Britain*; Diana Souhami's *Mrs Keppel and Her Daughter*; Raymond Lamont-Brown's *Edward VII's Last Loves*; A. J. P. Taylor's *The Struggle for Mastery in Europe, 1848–1918*; Chris Hutchins's and Peter Thompson's *Diana's Nightmare*; Andrew Morton's *Diana: Her True Story – In Her Own Words*; Dennis Friedman's *Ladies of the Bedchamber*; Vita Sackville-West's *The Edwardians*; Nigel Nicolson's *Portrait of a Marriage*; Roger Powell's *Royal Sex*; John Ashdown-Hill's *Royal Marriage Secrets*; Janice Hadlow's *The Strangest Family: The Private Lives of George III, Queen Charlotte and the Hanoverians*; Anne Edwards's *Matriarch: Queen Mary and the House of Windsor*; Sonia Keppel's *Edwardian Daughter*; Simon Heffer's *High Minds: The Victorians and the Birth of Modern Britain*; F. M. L. Thompson's *The Rise of Respectable Society: A Social History of Victorian Britain, 1830–1900*; Robert Ensor's *England, 1870–1914*; Roy Hattersley's *The Edwardians*, Princess Alice, Countess of Athlone's *For My Grandchildren*.

I've also drawn on my own previously published books, *Backstairs Billy: The Life of William Tallon, the Queen Mother's Most Devoted Servant* (published by Biteback) and *The Maid's Tale* (published by Hodder). Other books and sources are acknowledged throughout this book.

I owe a special debt of gratitude to the late Agnes Cook for bringing the past so marvellously to life, and to former domestic servants Rose Plummer and Nancy Jackman. A special thank you to Lady Wadham of Walberswick for steering me through the complexities of life in the grand manner.

I'd also like to thank the staff of the British Library for patiently guiding me through that institution's enormous collection of Victorian and Edwardian newspapers.

Last, but by no means least, thanks to Laurie De Decker at Biteback for patiently untangling all the knots and making sense of the muddles.